Choosing
Against War

A CHRISTIAN VIEW

"A Love Stronger Than Our Fears"

JOHN D. ROTH

Intercourse, PA 17534
800/762-7171
www.goodbks.com

ACKNOWLEDGMENTS

All biblical citations not credited to another translation are from the New Revised Standard Version Bible, copyright © 1989, by the Division of Christian Education of the National Council of the Churches of Christ in the United States of America. Used by permission. All rights reserved.

When the initials "NIV" follow citation, scripture taken from the HOLY BIBLE, NEW INTERNATIONAL VERSION®. NIV®. Copyright © 1973, 1978, 1984 by International Bible Society. Used by permission of Zondervan. All rights reserved.

When the initials "RSV" follow citation, scripture taken from the Revised Standard Version of the Bible. Copyright © 1952 [2nd edition, 1971] by the Division of Christian Education of the National Council of the Churches of Christ in the United States of America. Used by permission. All rights reserved.

The stanza of the song lyric on page 8 is copyrighted © 1995 WGRG, Iona Community, Glasgow, Scotland, G2 3DH. Words: John Bell. Received: From "Come all you people." Used by permission.

The lines of poetry on page 197 are from "The Second Coming" by W.B. Yeats. Reprinted with the permission of Scribner, an imprint of Simon & Schuster Adult Publishing Group, from THE COLLECTED WORKS OF W.B. YEATS, VOLUME 1: THE POEMS REVISED, edited by Richard J. Finneran. Copyright © 1924 by The Macmillan Company; copyright renewed © 1956 by Bertha Georgie Yeats.

Cover illustration by Allan Eitzen.
Design by Dawn J. Ranck

CHOOSING AGAINST WAR: A CHRISTIAN VIEW
Copyright © 2002 by Good Books, Intercourse, PA 17534
International Standard Book Number: 1-56148-359-1
Library of Congress Catalog Card Number: 2002073852

Library of Congress Cataloging-in-Publication Data
Roth, John D.,
    Choosing against war : a Christian view : a love stronger than our fears
/ John D. Roth.
    p. cm.
    Includes bibliographical references.
    ISBN 1-56148-359-1
    1. Pacifism--Religious aspects--Christianity. I. Title.
BT736.4.R66 2002
261.8'73--dc21   2002073852

TABLE OF CONTENTS

INTRODUCTION

L ate one evening, while attending a conference in the German city of Hamburg, I boarded a commuter train and headed for an outlying suburb where I was planning to spend the night. The train car was completely empty at that late hour, and I dozed sleepily as it rattled past the harbor and then through the industrial district. Some minutes into the trip, however, my reverie was sharply interrupted when an elderly man, dressed in rags and clearly suffering from a mental disability, shuffled into the car, closely followed by four teenagers. The young men, sporting an assortment of chains, tattoos, and body piercings, entered the car amid raucous laughter and loud talk. Almost immediately their attention focused on the old man who had seated himself near the center doors.

As I watched uneasily, the four began to taunt him, shouting obscenities and making humiliating references to his mental condition. Then one of the teens shook up a half-filled can of beer and aimed the foamy spray directly into the old man's face. Without warning, their verbal abuse suddenly escalated into a physical attack as they began kicking his legs with their heavy boots and punching him in the arms and face.

Seated toward the back of the car, I looked on with a mixture of horror and fear as the terrible scene unfolded before me. I am not a big person; I am not trained in any of the martial arts; I have never considered myself particu-

---

larly brave. Even more crucially, I have been a professing Christian for most of my adult life, and I have always understood pacifism to be at the very core of the good news of the gospel. Yet I knew with absolute certainty that I could not simply sit back and watch this helpless old man be mercilessly beaten.

As the seconds ticked past, a hundred different thoughts and emotions raced through my mind. I was angry—more than angry, really. I was enraged. This kind of violence was absolutely wrong! The old man had done nothing to deserve this kind of treatment.

Even more powerful than my anger, though, was a palpable sense of fear that overwhelmed me, a fear deep enough to taste. I have lived virtually all my life in the relative comfort and security of a small town where incidents of personal violence are nearly always limited to barroom brawls or domestic disputes, neither of which had ever directly affected me. Moreover, despite my longstanding commitment to peacemaking, nothing in my years of Sunday school classes in a pacifist denomination had prepared me to respond to such a situation. If I jumped in, what would keep them from attacking me? If they did assault me, would I try to defend myself? Did they have weapons? Were they drunk enough to kill us? There was no one else in the car to turn to for help, and the next stop was still several miles away.

Anger. Fear. Helplessness. These were the same emotions that gripped an entire nation—indeed, much of the world—when two hijacked passenger planes exploded violently into the World Trade Center buildings on the morning of September 11, 2001. In stunned disbelief and horror we looked on as the Hollywood-esque ball of orange flame burst out of the south tower. And then, before our eyes, we witnessed the cataclysmic collapse of the two buildings and the instantaneous death of more than 3,000 innocent people.

In the aftermath of those terrible scenes, as letters filled with anthrax spores threatened to paralyze government offices and rumors of additional terrorist targets dominated the media, that same anger and fear, along with an unfamiliar new sense of vulnerability, became nearly all-consuming. Suddenly, the comfortable patterns of daily life—activities as routine as flying in an airplane or opening the mail—had become fraught with danger. Our basic sense of security and freedom, once taken for granted, now seemed imperiled. Overnight, so it seemed, America found itself at war with an enemy it could scarcely identify, an enemy whose goals and convictions seemed as mysterious as they were destructive.

In the midst of these swirling fears, the American people struggled to find an adequate response to this confusing new world. For many, the first impulse was to call friends and family, to seek reassurance in the familiar voices and living presence of those closest to us. As time went by, however, our deep-seated fears began to find other forms of expression. One reaction, of course, was an outpouring of patriotic fervor. In moments of crisis, groups inevitably rally around their most powerful symbols of identity. For most Americans in the weeks following September 11, that symbol was clearly the flag. In communities across the United States, Americans joined in parades and vigils; they mounted flags on buildings, sidewalks, and cars; they posted slogans and signs; and they sang patriotic songs, all to reaffirm a collective sense of national identity and unity.

At the same time, Americans also squelched their fears by demanding that the violence of terrorism be resisted by the righteous violence of vengeance—or at the very least, the strong hand of justice. Within days of the attack one person in my community prominently displayed a 4x8 sheet of plywood with a hand-painted sign reading "Nuke the Bastards." Using slightly more moderate language, President Bush announced that America was resolved "to smoke the terrorists out of their holes" and he proclaimed the beginning of "the first war of the twenty-first century"—one launched against terrorists wherever they were to be found. Meanwhile, editorial columns in national and local newspapers called on the American people to unite unhesitatingly in the war effort and quickly branded all dissenting voices as being on par with the terrorists themselves.

> "If it is possible, so far as it depends on you, live peaceably with all."
> Romans 12:18

Such responses are certainly understandable. Anyone who has taken an introductory psychology course knows that most people, when threatened, usually resort either to "flight or fight." In the face of such horrific violence, it is not surprising that most Americans chose to circle the wagons, to rally the troops, and to brace themselves for a long and bloody war.

There was, however, still one other general response to the violence of September 11 that cannot be overlooked. In addition to expressing sentiments of patriotism and outrage, Americans also responded to their fear by turning to religion. In the week following the attacks, Bible sales across the United States increased by 27%, church attendance jumped by 6%, and thousands of people who had not been in church since their wedding days found themselves asking for God's blessing on America with just as much fervor as their deeply Christian neighbors.[1] When we feel most vulnerable our attention often turns to basic questions about life's meaning and our ultimate destiny. In times of crisis we turn to God.

The terrible events of September 11 thus offered the Christian church a significant occasion to respond to the nation with a distinctive voice. In the middle of suffering and death, when all of our easy assumptions about life are suddenly scrambled, Christians should be prepared to offer a unique, transformative perspective on the world—one fundamentally different from the hardwired response of "fight or flight," or the generic opinions of the workplace, media, or local bar.

At a time of widespread and profound fear, when the impulsive reaction of the nation is toward patriotic unity and an outrage bent on vengeance, what is the meaning of the "good news" of the gospel? Does the church—as the visible body of Christ, composed of Christians from around the world—have any unique insights on the problems of violence, terrorism, and warfare?

This book is written out of a conviction that the gospel of Jesus Christ does indeed speak to the crises of our day with a perspective that is both distinctive and unique. On the Sunday morning following the events of September 11, my small congregation in Indiana, along with millions of other Christians around the world, gathered for a service of worship, reflection, and remembrance. At a time when political pundits of every sort were groping for an appropriate response from the perspective of the nation, we asked God for help in understanding the events of the world from a divine perspective.

How, in the grand sweep of God's actions in history, should we respond to our new sense of fear and vulnerability? What might Christ have to teach us about the painful reality of violence and suffering in our world? During the course of our service, we shared many songs, thoughts, prayers, and admonitions. But the memory that has lingered with me the longest, looping repeatedly through my mind in the weeks that followed, was a fragment of a song whose text comes from the Iona community in Scotland:

Don't be afraid. My love is stronger.
My love is stronger than your fear.
Don't be afraid. My love is stronger,
And I have promised, promised to be always near.

To be sure, there is nothing particularly new or profound in the words of the song. After all, trust in God is the very foundation of Christian faith. The scriptures are full of admonitions to put our faith in Christ, to rely on God alone, to cast aside our fears in the knowledge of God's presence and strength. Yet if we were to take these words seriously, the declaration that "God's love is stronger than our fear" might actually turn out to have consequences far more profound than we might generally think.

How might Christians look on the world differently, if we actually—literally—believed that God's love was indeed stronger than our fears? What would happen if we assumed that our allegiance to God, our identity with Christ, and our commitment to the church would call us to respond to the world's pain differently than our non-Christian neighbors? In the face of violence, are there any options open to the Christian believer other than the default impulse toward patriotic unity and a steely determination to exact "an eye for an eye"?

This book is an effort to explore such a possibility. At one level, it is a straightforward argument that the gospel of Jesus Christ should lead all Christians to renounce violence and to love all human beings, including our enemies, with the same generous love that God has shown to us. At an even deeper level, it is an invitation to live more fully and joyfully in the Christian conviction that "God's love is stronger than our fears."

Which brings me back to my train car in the outskirts of Hamburg and the ugly scene of violence that was unfolding in front of me.

This is what I remember from the next few minutes of that drama. As the teenagers began to kick and pummel the old man, I whispered a deep prayer: "God, calm my fear. Show me the right thing to do." And then, without really giving my next actions any careful thought, I got out of my seat and walked purposefully toward the old man and his attackers. "Hans!" I called out in my best German, "Hans, how are you? It's been such a long time since we've seen each other!" And then, slipping between two of the surprised young men, I embraced him, helped him to his feet and said, "Come sit with me, Hans. We have so much to catch up on."

In the sudden silence that ensued, the old man followed me toward the rear of the car, slid into the window seat, and slowly, haltingly, began to respond to my onslaught of questions about his health and his family. The teens looked on, not sure how they should respond. For a time they talked among themselves. But when the train pulled into the next stop, they got out. And at the following stop, "Hans" left as well, mumbling a word of thanks.

A love that is stronger than our fear. The common sense of our culture teaches that the only way to respond to fear is a cowardly retreat or a fight to the finish. The beauty and power of the gospel, by contrast, is that Jesus Christ offers a third alternative: trust in God—and in the transforming, surprising, power of love.

This book is an invitation to consider the consequences of living more consistently in the living reality of God's love. Chapter One looks at the recent popularity of the phrase "What Would Jesus Do?" especially among evangelical Christians. Throughout the centuries Christians have been tempted to avoid this simple question by redefining faith as a list of doctrinal beliefs or as a private, personal relationship with God or as membership in a particular church. Yet followers of Jesus—those who bear the name of Christ—are called to be his disciples. In a world filled with violence, the question "What Would Jesus Do?" cannot help but bring us face to face with Christ's clear and consistent teachings on love, a love that extends even to the enemy.

> "The fruit of silence
> is prayer,
> The fruit of prayer
> is faith,
> The fruit of faith
> is love,
> The fruit of love
> is service,
> The fruit of service
> is peace."
> Mother Teresa

Chapter Two addresses some foundational questions related to our deepest assumptions about reality—our worldview. Many, perhaps most, people are quite ready to affirm the ideal of sacrificial love. Most would shudder at the thought of killing another human being and might even affirm, in principle at least, the merits of Christian nonviolence. Yet at the same time, there is a powerful temptation in our culture to insist that ultimately some form of coercive violence is necessary for good to prevail over evil. Sunday morning talk about loving the enemy is fine, but "realists" know deep down that at the end of the day the power of the fist (or the sword or gun or bomb) is really the universal solvent. Though such a worldview might sound compelling, I suggest that it is a perspective in which God becomes virtually irrelevant. A worldview that assumes that reality is ultimately based on coercion and force is literally a-theistic and one, therefore, that Christians should want to challenge.

In the following chapter, I propose an alternative narrative about reality, a worldview deeply rooted in the biblical account of Creation, the Fall, and God's tireless efforts at redemption. Christians of all persuasions affirm that human beings were created to live in Shalom—that is, to live in harmony with God, with each other, and with nature.

In the story of the Fall, the Shalom for which we were meant has been shattered. But the great power of the Christian story is its dramatic account of God's stubborn determination to call human beings back to the purpose for which we were originally created. In Christ, we have both the means and the model of Shalom's restoration. The church, Christ's body made visible to the world, offers a living testimony to the power of God's Shalom and the ultimate victory of the resurrection over the competing claims of violence and death.

Chapter Four expands on one specific theme of the non-violent power of the cross: humility. Far from encouraging a passive retreat from the world, humility seeks to embody the vulnerability of the cross in everyday human relations. For the Christian, humility includes a willingness to give up control over the outcome of history; it refuses to ground Christian faith in the coercive logic of the debater; it confesses that our ethical actions are not always consistent; and it seeks to listen with special care to the voices of our opponents. In the end, Christian pacifism is not an argument to be won, or a tool for reaching ideal political outcomes, or even an airtight ethical system. It is simply a commitment to follow Jesus sincerely and completely, even if that path should lead to the cross.

In Chapter Five I attempt to address head-on the tensions Christians sometimes feel between faith in God and their sense of loyalty to the nation. At the heart of this tension is a fundamental question regarding our basic allegiance. Does our identity rest primarily in the bonds of patriotic loyalty to a particular nation, or do our commitments to Christ call us to a higher allegiance whose boundaries transcend those of the nation-state?

Choosing against war is not merely a moral decision made in the context of armed conflict. A consistent form of Christian pacifism may also nudge believers in peacetime to be cautious about accepting the notion of a "Christian nation," and it may prompt Christians to think more critically about the meaning of patriotism. Chapter Five concludes with an effort to respond to some of the criticisms frequently raised against the commitment to Christian pacifism.

Finally, because Christian pacifists often have a reputation for being clearer about what they are *against* rather than what they actually *affirm*, Chapter Six concludes with some examples of how Christians committed to the gospel of peace are putting their faith into action. Christian citizens, I suggest, should be politically engaged—not primarily in the traditional sense of party politics and partisan lobbying, but in more creative and transformative ways that remain true to the principles of Christian love and humility. Christian citizens will actively promote the quality of life in their communities by living lives of personal integrity, by nurturing the dignity and well-being of their neighbors, by fostering perspectives that transcend national borders, and by bearing witness in word and deed to the promise of God's Shalom.

One final thought: a life lived in dependence on God offers no predictable outcomes or guarantees of physical safety. This book will not argue that pacifism always "works," in the sense of bringing about a resolution to conflict in which the aggressor inevitably backs down. Indeed, my story could also have ended with the teenagers beating up both of us. History is filled with accounts of Christians whose faith and trust in God resulted in their deaths. But we remember them as martyrs precisely because they died in the confidence of a love more powerful than fear. With the apostle Paul, Christians proclaim a Christ who demonstrated that "power is made perfect in weakness" (2 Corinthians 12:9). Our calling is to live with joy in the power of that love.

---

[1] *Christianity Today* (November 12, 2001), 19.

1.

"WHAT WOULD JESUS DO?" — ON BEING A CHRISTIAN IN NORTH AMERICA

"Most of Christ's teachings disagree with our way of living. But preachers, . . . seeing that men will not fit their ways to Christ's pattern, have fitted His teaching to human customs, to get agreement somehow or other."
Thomas More, *Utopia* **(1516)**

In 1896 novelist Charles M. Sheldon published a book that captured the enduring attention of Christian readers for generations to come. *In His Steps* tells the story of a small-town, Protestant congregation somewhere in the Midwest. Early in the book a mysterious stranger, a tramp dressed in rags, disturbs the neatly ordered life of the parishioners of First Church by interrupting their singing one Sunday morning with a request for help. When the well-heeled members reject his plea, the tramp exclaims to the congregation, "It seems to me there's an awful lot of trouble in the world that somehow wouldn't exist if all the people who sing such songs went and lived them out." And then, without warning, he lurches over the communion table and dies on the spot, leaving the stunned congregation to sort through its response.

As it turns out, the disruptive event sparks a revival at First Church. Led by pastor Henry Maxwell, several members of the congregation pledge to structure their lives for an entire year around the simple question: what would Jesus do?

That question, and their determination to respond to it with integrity, ultimately transforms the entire congregation. In seeking to follow Jesus concretely—in deed as well as in word—the congregation finds itself pulled out of the comfort of its traditional piety into the messy and painful realities of urban life in Chicago. Within a year, spiritual revival becomes inextricably linked to social reform, and the book ends with Maxwell and his parishioners deeply involved in the daily lives and local neighborhoods of those they have come to serve.

Nearly a hundred years later, a youth group at Calvary Reformed Church in Holland, Michigan, read Sheldon's novel and was inspired to shape their lives around the same question: what would Jesus do? To remind themselves of this commitment they began to wear homemade bracelets with the letters "WWJD" woven into them. The bracelets quickly aroused the curiosity of their classmates and friends, and before long the WWJD movement had spread throughout the entire nation. Today, an estimated 14 million bracelets have been sold and the WWJD campaign has gone mainstream, appearing on hundreds of products. The official WWJD website calls the phenomenon "a counter-cultural revolution that has reverberated around the world."

What would Jesus do? The question certainly sounds simple and uncontroversial enough. After all, it seems obvious that those who claim the name of Christ would want to pattern their lives around his teaching and example. Obvious, that is, until you leave the safety of a Sunday morning worship service and start to ask what this might actually mean in the routines of daily life during the rest of the week.

The moment you start to get specific about what all is implied in doing what Jesus would do, the question suddenly becomes much more complicated. After all, we are likely to say, Jesus lived in a very different cultural context—the issues he faced in first-century Palestine are not the same as those we encounter in the twenty-first century. Would Jesus run for public office or lobby for political causes? Would Jesus defend his mother if she were attacked? Would Jesus avoid movies rated "R" for violence? The Gospels simply do not address these questions, at least not directly.

The basic sentiment is clear enough: Christians all want to follow Jesus. But the more concretely we try to answer the question, what would Jesus do?, the more uncomfortable we are with the possible implications of the answers. Fearful, perhaps, that taking the WWJD question seriously might challenge comfortable assumptions and habits, we prefer not to linger too long on the question. And so it seems that many contemporary Christians, even those who prominently display the WWJD motto, are more inclined to avoid the question, to evade hard thinking about the concrete teachings and example of Jesus and, instead, to reformulate the essence of Christian faith in terms that are more amendable to our current cultural practices.

Consider, for example, five varieties of Christian faith commonly practiced today. Each offers the world some very important truths about the essence of Christianity. None is a false or heretical form of Christian faith. And almost never do these expressions of faith consciously try to avoid following Christ in daily life. But in their own distinct way, each version of Christianity has found a means of blunting the difficult challenge posed by the WWJD question.

To the extent that each implies that WWJD is not really central to the good news of the gospel, it offers an incomplete perspective on biblical faith.

Not WWJD, But the *Cross* Is What Really Matters

Perhaps the most common way we can avoid the challenge to live as Jesus did is to shift our focus from his life and teachings to his death and resurrection. Of course Jesus did lots of good things while he was alive, but the real purpose of his life was not what he said or did, but that he died on the cross so that we could enjoy the gift of salvation. In sending Jesus to the world, God's intention was to provide sinful humanity with a means of satisfying the debt of our guilt before God. Thus, Jesus came to earth as a completely sinless and innocent person.

On our behalf he shed his blood and died a painful death, and because he did this, God can grant each of us the gift of grace and eternal life. Therefore, the question is not really "What would Jesus do?" but "What *did* Jesus do?" Jesus has already accomplished his mission; all we need to do now is to confess our sins and accept the sacrifice he made on our behalf. Of course Christians should strive to be good people, but the real drama of salvation has already happened on the cross. This should be our focus: giving thanks to God for His grace, and then inviting other people to enjoy the free gift of salvation.

Not WWJD, But *Doctrine* Is What Really Matters

For some contemporary Christians, Christian faith essentially boils down to the life of the mind, that is, to matters of belief. Through the ages, gifted church leaders and theologians have studied the Bible carefully, have debated the nature of salvation from every possible angle, and have formulated a series of specific statements that seem to distill accurately and precisely the essence of Christian theology. To become a Christian usually means that you have given these questions careful thought, and then have answered—often in the form of a public statement or affirmations to questions—"yes," you do indeed believe these statements to be true. To be sure, those who emphasize doctrinal beliefs would always insist on the importance of a relationship with God, and they would encourage Christians to live upright lives. But Christian faith takes on a tangible, concrete expression, it becomes visible and real, when the believer affirms a list of specific doctrines and then pledges to defend them with thoughtful arguments and careful proofs from Scripture.

> *"Blessed are the peacemakers, for they will be called children of God."*
> Matthew 5:9

Not WWJD, But *Feelings* Are What Really Matter

There are other modern Christians who are apt to say—or, more likely, to imply through their preaching and actions—that the essence of Christian faith can be found in the inward, personal, subjective experience that the believer has, once she has accepted Christ into her life as personal Savior. In this stream of Christianity, belief is not linked so much to a formal set of doctrines as it is to the emotional state of happiness, joy, and inner peace that accompanies God's presence in our lives.

Knowing that our moods can fluctuate, that there are times when we do not always sense the warm inner feeling of spiritual security, these Christians stress the importance of regular revival experiences, often accompanied by dramatic, emotional expressions of repentance or ecstatic joy.

Christians who emphasize the importance of feelings are likely to be critical of the academic abstractions that sometimes accompany an emphasis on doctrine; they are leery about a faith that is tied too closely to rules of ethical behavior. What matters most is the inner experience of the living presence of the Holy Spirit and a sense in your heart of God's intimacy and love.

Not WWJD, But *Membership* Is What Really Matters

Still other contemporary Christians suggest that the most important aspect of faith is a ritual of membership in which believers join the church and have their names inscribed into a heavenly "book of life." For those denominations that practice infant baptism, the act of membership occurs very early in life, while the individual is still a baby. Through baptism, God's grace and salvation are conferred on the child and he, in some sense, thereby becomes a Christian, regardless of his intentions or beliefs or feelings.

Sometimes the link between membership and salvation is less explicit. For some people raised in churches with strong family traditions or ethnic identity, faith becomes a kind of genealogical inheritance, a birthright you receive from a previous generation, with the assumption that you, in turn, are to pass it along to your children. Doctrine and feelings and behavior matter, of course, but the bedrock of Christian identity is the ritual of baptism and your membership in a particular church.

Not WWJD, But *Being Good* Is What Really Matters

Finally, there are many people who call themselves Christians largely because they conform to widely accepted and respectable standards of moral behavior. They may not invest a lot of energy in the finer points of doctrine; they are not likely to speak of an emotion-filled or personal relationship with Christ; they may not be all that vigilant in church attendance. But they are responsible and upstanding members of the community.

Such Christians do not cheat on their tax returns; they don't steal from their employees; they keep their lawns mowed and their leaves raked; they contribute to the United Way campaign; they serve on local school boards; they fly their flags on the Fourth of July; they obey the law; they are polite to their families and friends. These believers are pragmatic and matter-of-fact about faith. Jesus taught that Christians would be recognized by their fruits. In a world full of duplicity and greed, living as a decent, law-abiding citizen is evidence enough of one's personal religious convictions.

But What Would Jesus Do?

Clearly these short summaries are too brief to be fair to any single position. Many Christians would likely want to agree with some combination of these categories, and there are definitely positive aspects to each of these tendencies that enhance the Christian witness and could be defended on the basis of Scripture.

What is less clear, however, about any of these five categories is whether they offer a helpful understanding as to how we might model our lives more completely around the life and teaching of Jesus.

Surely the crucifixion was central to Jesus' mission on earth, but if this was the only reason he came, why did he spend so much time and energy teaching the disciples how they were to live? Or why did he warn that it would not be those who say "Lord, Lord" who will enter the Kingdom, but rather the one "who does the will of my Father" (Matthew 7:21)?

Surely Jesus cared about belief. "The one who believes," he told his listeners, "will be saved" (Mark 16:16). But he did not demand that his followers agree on a highly detailed list of doctrinal tenets before they could be considered his disciples.

Surely Jesus was a man of deep emotions who had close personal relations with a wide range of people. But he never suggested that following him would guarantee good, warm feelings or freedom from all doubts, uncertainties, and periods of confusion.

Surely Jesus cared about group identity—so much so, in fact, that he warned the disciples that allegiance to God could mean a painful separation from the natural bonds of affection they had with their biological families. But the decision to follow Jesus was never routine or automatic. Peter, James, and John *chose* to follow Jesus. No one was born a disciple.

And surely Jesus taught his followers to be good people—to be generous, compassionate, and responsible. But he also explicitly warned against those who thought discipleship could be reduced to following a code of common etiquette. Even the Pharisees and the righteous heathen, he said, love their neighbors and hate their enemies. There is nothing uniquely Christian about condemning adultery or demanding the justice of "an eye for an eye, and a tooth for a tooth." Good deeds certainly mattered to Jesus, but he seems to have been less interested in gathering around him good people than in inviting people to be transformed in every aspect of their lives.

So what *does* it mean to be a follower of Jesus? How *should* we respond to the question, "What would Jesus do?" To a large extent, the answers to these questions can only be sorted out in local settings with other Christian believers who are committed to discerning God's will for their lives in very specific and concrete ways. Christian faith is too dynamic, too adventurous, to be reduced to simple formulas or a fixed set of principles.

At the same time, however, the gospels do offer some very important insights into Christ's ministry that are worth pondering, especially for those who want to take the WWJD challenge seriously. The themes from Jesus' teachings and example that I want to highlight are not comprehensive. But they may provide a number of important clues for contemporary Christians to consider, especially those of us who are looking for a way to bring a new sense of vitality, joy, and relevance into our Christian lives.

Before turning to these themes, I want to identify briefly three basic principles that I will be assuming in the reflections concluding this chapter and in the rest of the book. If, as I hope will be the case, these convictions seem reasonable to those of you who are Christians, I invite you to enter with vigor into the discussion that follows. If, on the other hand, these convictions sound preposterous or you find them cluttered with doctrinal errors, then perhaps this book is not for you.

For those readers who do not profess Christianity, I hope that the exploration that follows on the WWJD question will nudge you to think further about your own convictions and that these reflections might point you to a new life in Christ.

Some Beginning Premises

1. This book assumes that the Bible offers a true account of God's work in history and God's desire for human beings—that it is a trustworthy basis for faith and life. To be sure, Christians have not always agreed about the proper interpretation of scripture, but they do share a conviction

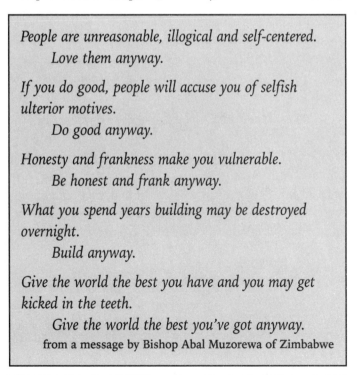

People are unreasonable, illogical and self-centered.
   Love them anyway.

If you do good, people will accuse you of selfish ulterior motives.
   Do good anyway.

Honesty and frankness make you vulnerable.
   Be honest and frank anyway.

What you spend years building may be destroyed overnight.
   Build anyway.

Give the world the best you have and you may get kicked in the teeth.
   Give the world the best you've got anyway.

from a message by Bishop Abal Muzorewa of Zimbabwe

that the Bible is the appropriate starting point for understanding God's will for humanity. In my reflections I will frequently refer to specific passages in scripture, trying to illuminate their relevance for our lives today. But even more crucial to my perspective are the broad, overarching themes in the biblical story, from Genesis to Revelation, that lie at the heart of a Christian understanding of reality.

2. At the center of the biblical account—the hinge on which the whole narrative turns—is the life, death, and resurrection of Jesus Christ. Christ reoriented human history so fundamentally that the Western tradition recalibrated its calendar in recognition of the cosmic significance of his birth. In Jesus Christ we find the fullest expression of God's character. Thus, if we want to understand who God is or what God is trying to do in the world, our focus should be on Christ's life and teachings. Christ not only offers forgiveness for our sins, but also extends an invitation to follow him in daily life. Indeed, one cannot truly know Christ apart from a commitment to live in accordance with Christ's teaching and example.

3. God's love for the world, expressed most fully in Christ, is genuinely good news, defying all human comprehension. God's love is *unmerited*, given without condition and without any demand that it be reciprocated. It is *vulnerable*, expressed in the form of a human being who renounced his own status, assumed the role of a servant, and willingly suffered humiliation, pain, and death. It is *irrational*, granted as freely to enemies as it is to friends. It is *empowering*, enabling all those who experience it to also, in turn, share it fully with others. And it is *persistent*, extended patiently and stubbornly even to those who choose to reject it. This is the good news of the gospel. God's love invites us to become "new creatures in

Christ"—people whose hearts are transformed, whose minds are renewed, whose very identity is reshaped by the forgiveness and compassion that has been extended to us. Our calling, as Christians, is to embody this same love in a world that has not yet been redeemed.

So What Would Jesus Do?

If these principles seem clear—or at least plausible—then we are ready to return to the question we started with: "What would Jesus do?"

Modern Christians looking for concrete answers to this simple question might begin by reflecting on the following five principles of joyful Christian discipleship. These five points do not exhaust the fullness of the Christian experience, nor are they an adequate summary of what it means to be a Christian. But they do suggest a framework for a practical Christian life—one that takes seriously the question WWJD and one that embraces the world with a love that is stronger than our fear.

1. See yourself as a participant in God's plan for human history.
In the gospel of Luke, Jesus began his public ministry in a rather dramatic fashion. As Luke relates the story, Jesus entered the local synagogue in Nazareth one Sabbath day and stood up to read a passage from the prophet Isaiah. "The Spirit of the Lord is upon me," he read, "because he has anointed me to bring good news to the poor. He has sent me to proclaim release to the captives and recovery of sight to the blind, to let the oppressed go free, to proclaim the year of the Lord's favor" (Luke 4:18-19). Those gathered in the synagogue had almost certainly heard these words from the prophet many times before. But what they had not heard before was the stunning claim Jesus made

when he was done reading, namely, that it was Jesus himself whom God had anointed to carry out these acts of healing and restoration. "Today," Jesus told his listeners in the synagogue, "this scripture has been fulfilled in your hearing" (Luke 4:21).

From the beginning of his ministry to his final transfiguration into heaven, Jesus understood everything that he taught and did to be part of a grand unfolding plan in which God's purposes were being revealed in history. Repeatedly, Jesus sought to link his teachings to the larger story of God's people. The 12 disciples he gathered around him, for example, echoed the 12 tribes of Israel, 10 of which had been lost to history but were now being restored. The Sermon on the Mount was not intended to be a new law, but a deeper and more profound understanding of the law given to Moses. Jesus himself was the fulfillment of the ancient prophecies that a Messiah would come to heal and restore a suffering people. The miracles of Christ were in deep continuity with God's miraculous intervention in the stories of the Old Testament. In short, it is impossible to understand the life and teachings of Jesus apart from a much broader narrative of God acting in history.

Modern Christians who are truly interested in following Jesus could take an important clue from this simple principle. We sometimes think that faith is something that we need to sit down and carefully figure out before we are ready go out and live Christian lives. What we can easily overlook is the fact that faith does not exist in some disembodied, abstract form. Like our own individual identities, faith is always embedded in a broader story line that shapes our deepest perspectives on the world.

At its heart, being a Christian is accepting God's invitation to participate in a grand story much bigger than ourselves, in which we claim a role in a drama that already has a coherent plotline. Like Jesus, we are called to find our place within this grand narrative and to become active participants in a story that began with Creation and is heading toward the joyful culmination of history in the Wedding Feast of the Lamb that John described in the Book of Revelation.

To be sure, our role in that drama is not always clear. We sometimes find ourselves at the very edge of the stage, or we momentarily forget our lines altogether. In the end, however, Christians are willing participants in a drama whose basic plotline has long been established, even as they continue to shape their own characters and roles in that unfolding story.

To answer the question "What would Jesus do?" we should start, like Jesus did, by understanding our lives in the perspective of God's grand narrative.

2. Live in the confident knowledge that God is more powerful than nature, humans, and death itself. Throughout his ministry Jesus consistently demonstrated the power of God in ways that defied human understanding. When a storm threatened to sink the boat he was in, Jesus commanded the winds to subside (Luke 8:22-25). When the blind and the lame, the deaf and the dumb, came to Jesus, he sent them away healed. When the only son of a widow died, Jesus restored him to life again (Luke 7:11-15). When Jesus himself faced the reality of a slow and painful death, God raised him up from the dead.

Over and over again, Jesus challenged the notion that reality could be reduced to what we can see, touch, measure, and predict. Beyond the perception of our senses and the obvious reality of common sense, Jesus pointed to an even deeper, spiritual reality that transcends our natural understanding. When Christians pray, we testify to this reality by acknowledging that God is ultimately in control of our world in ways that go beyond our comprehension.

To answer the question "What would Jesus do?" we should start, like Jesus did, by assuming that God's purposes frequently defy our commonsensical understandings of reality, bringing life and wholeness to situations that seem overwhelmed by the apparent finality of death.

3. *Practice extravagant generosity and hospitality, especially to those at the edges of society.* In the story of Jesus' birth, we get a glimpse of the kinds of people to whom Jesus' ministry will eventually be directed. Gathered around a manger in a cowshed, a motley group of Palestinian shepherds celebrated the birth of the Messiah. This baby, God in human flesh, grew up to start a renewal movement within Judaism that attracted people from every walk of life, but especially those who found themselves at the very edges of respectability. Included among the disciples were blue-collar fishermen, a white-collar tax collector, at least one revolutionary, and a host of other very ordinary people—in other words, a cross-section of Jewish society.

> "Christ with his blood
> gathers the army
> that sheds no blood . . .
> We Christians
> are a peaceful people,
> bred not for war
> but for peace."
> Clement of Alexandra

Along the way, Jesus made it a point to extend a special kind of compassion to prostitutes and criminals, to cheaters and children, to the mentally unbalanced and the physically deformed. In so doing, Jesus consistently surprised and upset the religious establishment of his time by suggesting that hospitality to the people on the margins of society offered a true picture of God's very nature.

To answer the question "What would Jesus do?" we should start, like Jesus did, by extending dignity and hospitality to those people society considers outside the bounds of respectable company.

4. *Teach with authority and courage.* In Jesus we discover a remarkable combination of humility and confidence. This long-awaited Messiah, this King of the Jews, mingled freely with common people and regularly called on his disciples to regard themselves as servants, not masters. And yet, at the same time, Jesus aroused the respect and the fear of his contemporaries in part, at least, because "he taught them as one having authority, and not as their scribes" (Matthew 7:29).

Here was a man deeply confident in his own sense of mission and destiny. With unswerving courage he spoke truth to the powers, both religious and political, never hesitating to confront injustice. Yet his manner of challenging those in authority often came in the form of a creative surprise, leaving his opponents bewildered about how to respond.

To those ready to kill a woman caught in adultery, Jesus challenged the one who was without sin to throw the first stone. When entrepreneurs threatened to turn God's temple into Wall Street, Jesus angered the establishment by dramatically overturning tables and creating a public scene. When Roman soldiers coerced Jews in occupied Israel to carry their bags for a mile, Jesus suggested that they might retain their dignity, and shame their oppressors, by carrying the bags for two miles.

Whereas much of American Christianity has focused on

the personal nature of Christ's role in our lives, Jesus' ministry always had a clear public, even political, component that was troubling to those in power. He was disturbing not because he wanted to claim that power for himself, but because he modeled an alternative form of power that authorities found very unsettling.

To answer the question "What would Jesus do?" we should start, like Jesus did, by witnessing in courageous and creative ways that may challenge the assumptions of those in power.

5. Live a life of nonviolent love, even if it means humiliation, suffering, or death. A biblical scholar once described the gospels as "passion narratives with long introductions." What he meant was that the stories we have of Jesus' life—his teachings and his actions—play themselves out in the course of a three-year journey that was headed, slowly but surely, toward Jerusalem and his eventual crucifixion and death.

All along the way, Jesus tried to help his disciples understand the paradoxical nature of his kingship. "Whoever wishes to be great among you must be your servant" (Matthew 20:26), he told his disciples when he found them arguing over who was the greatest. When he entered Jerusalem in a moment of glory just before his execution, Jesus rode a humble donkey, not a white stallion of war. On the night of his betrayal, Jesus stooped to wash the feet of his disciples. Even in the midst of excruciating pain on the cross, Jesus refused to give in to hatred but instead asked God to forgive those who were persecuting him.

He did all this not because he was a masochist or because he was a coward. Rather, Jesus sought to embody the true nature of God's love in his own life—a love offered freely, without conditions or restrictions, to everyone, including those who were seeking to kill him.

Christian faith is relevant to the world, therefore, just to the extent that it is capable of responding to evil and violence in a genuinely Christ-like manner. For the Christian, violence is the crucible where doubts are smelted into faith and fear is transformed into love. Though it may seem foolish to the world, Christians love their enemies and do good to those who would harm them precisely because they live in the knowledge of the resurrection and the certainty that life in God will ultimately triumph over the power of death.

To answer the question "What would Jesus do?" we should start, like Jesus did, by loving others fully and vulnerably—even at the risk of humiliation, suffering, and death itself—because we know that, in the end, the power of love and life will trump the forces of death.

When Henry Maxwell and his congregation decided to shape their lives as much as possible around the example of Jesus, their lives did not suddenly become simpler. To ask "What would Jesus do?" will inevitably bring Christian believers face to face with numerous complex questions of interpretation and discernment, of courage and commitment, of failure and forgiveness. Undoubtedly, there will be times when the challenge to live like Jesus will seem hopelessly impossible.

But Christians throughout the ages have steadfastly given witness to the fact that Jesus not only came as a cosmic Savior to free us from our sins, he also came to offer an example of God's love and God's deepest purposes for humanity. The grace that forgives our sins also enables us to become new creatures in Christ.

2.

REALISM OR IDEALISM?

"For the message about the cross is foolishness to those who are perishing, but to us who are being saved it is the power of God . . . . Where is the one who is wise? Where is the scribe? Where is the debater of this age? Has not God made foolish the wisdom of the world? . . . Jews demand signs and Greeks desire wisdom, but we proclaim Christ crucified, a stumbling block to Jews and foolishness to Gentiles, but to those who are called, both Jews and Greeks, Christ the power of God and the wisdom of God. For God's foolishness is wiser than human wisdom, and God's weakness is stronger than human strength."

I Corinthians 1:18-25

The political cartoon was simple; its point immediately clear. Sketched in the background was the New York City skyline and the still-smoldering ruins of the World Trade Center buildings. Dominating the foreground of the picture was a large ostrich, its head buried deeply in the sand. The only caption on the cartoon was a simple label on the ostrich that read: "the anti-war movement."

The barbed message is an ancient one, repeated so frequently that it almost seems to be a truism: pacifists are simply out of touch with reality.

On the surface, the argument sounds convincing enough. Few people in our society would suggest that violence is a good thing. But it seems equally clear to most people, including many Christians, that as long as criminals and crazy people are running loose in the world, a certain amount of violence is inevitable—at least if innocent people are to be protected.

Essentially, goes the reasoning, anyone who rejects violence or challenges the logic of war is politically naïve and morally irresponsible. Like the ostrich in the cartoon, such people choose to be willfully ignorant about the reality of evil. They think that war criminals and sexual predators will somehow be magically transformed into upright citizens if only we are nice to them. They hope that terrorists will be dissuaded from planting bombs if we just extend the olive branch of kindness.

By contrast, responsible citizens, according to this point of view, are much more realistic. They know that violence is the only language evildoers understand. And because they live in the real world rather than a world of idealistic fantasies, they take threats of wrongful violence seriously and are willing to respond with force if necessary in order to preserve the larger principles of freedom and goodness.

The argument is compelling. It appeals to our most basic instincts (self-defense); it accords well with common-sense notions of justice ("an eye for an eye and a tooth for a tooth"); and it seems to be borne out by the weight of history (appeasing aggressors only encourages more evil).

What is not clear in the argument, however—and it is a crucial missing piece—is how this presumably logical and commonsensical response to violence can be squared with the gospel of Jesus Christ. Do arguments that justify killing—even if your cause is sufficiently righteous—correctly answer the question "What would Jesus do?"

The Power of a Worldview

Unless you have struggled with mental illness or happen to be employed as a philosopher, you probably have not spent a lot of time thinking about whether the world as you experience it is real or not. You may have given a lot of thought to what you believe, or the code of ethics by which you wish to live, but most of us do not agonize very consciously about the nature of reality itself.

Yet from the moment of our births, our understanding of the world—its structure and order—is profoundly shaped by the languages we speak, by the homes and families in which we are raised, by the subtle pressures of our peer groups, and by the many assumptions that are deeply embedded in our cultural understandings of gender, race, class, and even religion. Our individual perspectives—our worldviews—have tremendous power, in part because they present the world to us in terms that seem obvious and inevitable. Like fish in water, we are often so immersed in our basic assumptions about the nature of reality that we can scarcely recognize those outside forces that are actively shaping our understanding of how the world works.

Our worldviews must be taken seriously because they ultimately shape our daily actions and ethical behavior. Although we may self-consciously challenge certain of our attitudes—racist assumptions, for example, or unthinking prejudices against people with disabilities—we are probably not actually going to *act* any differently, at least not consistently, unless something changes in our basic worldview. Thus, we may publicly espouse certain principles or cherish certain ideals, but our concrete actions usually provide a much better window into our actual worldview than these public statements or claims.

For Christians, the question of our worldview is of utmost importance precisely because it calls attention to our deepest assumptions about the nature of reality. Of course, as I suggested in Chapter One, there are some Christians who would argue that faith is primarily a question of getting your doctrine straight or going to the right church or feeling happy or simply becoming a good, decent person. If pressed, however, most Christians would assert that faith is something deeper than all this.

At its heart, Christian faith points toward a transformed understanding of reality itself. In Christian language, repentance or conversion implies a fundamental "turning around." It begins with a recognition that our natural ways of making sense of the world are deeply skewed, and it calls us to reorient our entire perspective in the new light of Christ's living, transforming presence in the world.

Exactly what all is implied in this reorientation—the specific form Christian faith assumes in daily life—will be explored in more detail later. What is important for the moment is the simple point that Christian faith implies a fundamental change in our worldview—a realignment of our deepest understandings and assumptions regarding the nature of reality and, consequently, a new way of living that corresponds to this reformulated perspective.

Such a realignment of perspective, of course, is not an easy thing. Old habits and assumptions die very hard. In seeking to conform ourselves to the spirit of Christ we don't always get it right. Indeed, at the heart of the Christian life is a deepening understanding of how living in the presence of God's reality challenges and transforms every aspect of our daily lives. But this is the high calling of the Christian disciple—and it is a calling to a life of true joy.

In this chapter I want to explore more carefully the nature of our worldview, focusing especially on the meaning of the word "realism." Christians, I believe, are called to live actively in the *real* world. They are not to hide their faces from the pain, violence, and brokenness that is all too evident in daily life. But because they see that world from a divine perspective, from the vantage point of Christian faith, they will be cautious about accepting uncritically the standard definitions of what is real, even though those definitions may seem commonsensical and are widely shared by the broader culture.

In taking this position, I do not pretend to be saying anything new. When Jesus said "the first shall be last" or "you must become as children to enter into the Kingdom of Heaven," he was calling his disciples to see the world from a new perspective. When the apostle Paul cautioned the church at Rome not to be "conformed to this world," he was calling them to live in tension with notions of truth that were simply assumed in the broader culture (Romans 12:2). When he later wrote to the church at Corinth that Greeks would reject the notion of a "crucified Christ" as "foolishness" and Jews would regard it as a "stumbling block," he was expressing precisely the same point (I Corinthians 1:23).

The gospel preached by both Jesus and Paul is genuinely "good news." It is a liberating vision of a deeper and truer reality than that assumed by the world. What makes that gospel truly good and genuinely newsworthy becomes apparent only when it is contrasted with the false reality of the world. It is to that diagnosis that we now turn.

The Nature of Reality – A Nietzschean (Modern) Worldview

More than a hundred years ago a German philosopher by the name of Friedrich Nietzsche gained enduring notoriety with his announcement that "God is dead!" Nietzsche actually put these words in the mouth of an insane man who lit a lantern in broad daylight and then rushed into a crowded marketplace shouting, "I seek God! I seek God!" The people around him began to scoff. "Is God lost?" asked someone. "Is he hiding?" asked another. "Did he lose his way?" "Is he afraid of us?" As the people taunted the madman, he turned on them and shouted angrily: "God is dead, I tell you, we have killed him, you and I! All of us are his murderers!"[1]

Nietzsche's proclamation of God's death undoubtedly sounds odd to most modern Christians. Despite a short-lived resurgence of popularity in the late 1960s among secular skeptics and some liberal theologians, the death of God is seldom spoken about seriously today. "God is not dead," we are likely to retort along with a bumper sticker popular in the 1970s, "I just talked with Him this morning!"

Yet at a deeper level, the haunting claim of Nietzsche's madman has proven to be an apt description of contemporary culture. Writing at the end of the nineteenth century, Nietzsche looked on the Christian church in Europe and found it to be a hollow shell, a cultural institution of the European middle class that demanded the social conformity of its members but was utterly lacking in any spiritual vitality. And with good reason, Nietzsche argued, since

Christianity itself was an elaborate hoax, a servile religion premised on weak-kneed notions of forgiveness and love that had duped the common people into giving up their freedom and autonomy.

The Sermon on the Mount, he claimed, was a gospel worthy of sheep. It promoted meekness in the face of power, passivity in the face of oppression, and patient suffering in the face of threats to one's property and personal security. Modern people, he argued, should be able to see through this veil of ignorance and have the courage to admit publicly that God is no longer relevant to human affairs.

Power, not compassion, Nietzsche argued, is the true motor of history. The real heroes of the modern age are those brave individuals, the "supermen" (*Übermenschen*), willing to renounce the artificial constraints of tradition, morality, and law, to lay sentimentality aside, and to shape the future by bravely wielding the tools of raw coercive power.

To be sure, such a brazen appeal to sheer power sounds chilling to our ears. "If God is dead," wrote the Russian novelist Dostoyevsky, "then everything is possible," including, as the history of the twentieth century has amply demonstrated, the horrific deeds of Adolf Hitler, Josef Stalin, Mao Tse Tung and Pol Pot.

Surely no one today, least of all those in the Christian church, would want to defend such a worldview or live in a society where such notions were commonplace. After all, our nation was founded on Christian principles, our laws reflect the guiding motifs of the Ten Commandments, we have more churches per square mile than any other country in the world, and, according to recent polls, more than 90% of Americans continue to believe in God. Like the pedestrians in the marketplace of Nietzsche's fable, we are apt to scoff at anyone crass enough to announce that "God is dead," or to dismiss such claims as evil and subversive.

And yet, to a disturbing degree, much of contemporary American culture is premised on a worldview that shares many of Nietzsche's assumptions—not explicitly, perhaps, but in more subtle and sanitized forms that have a profound influence on how Christians actually live and what they teach their children. Although few Christians would ever consciously defend these ideas, naming them may alert us to the way in which we may have unwittingly adopted a perspective on life that is actually quite alien to a genuinely Christian worldview.

> *"Jesus said, 'My kingdom is not of this world. If it were, my servants would fight. . .'"*
> John 18:36 (NIV)

The Triumph of a Nietzschean Worldview?

Consider, for example, the following claims characteristic of a worldview based on the Nietzschean assumption that God is dead:

1. *Life is an endless struggle for power. To the victor go the rewards.* If we are sufficiently honest and insightful about human history, we will recognize that life ultimately boils down to an unceasing battle of competing interests in which the rewards ultimately go to the powerful. Of course, most of us are somewhat squeamish about such a bare-knuckles understanding of human relations.

We would much prefer to use the language of religious convictions or patriotic ideals to describe our actions when faced with competing interests. And we are likely to disguise the raw nature of coercive force in society by hiding it behind our financial resources, our privileged access to information, our seats on corporate boards, or our control of technology. But underneath all of the high-minded appeals to principles and the chameleon-like forms that power assumes, life in the end comes down to the survival of the fittest.

Television game shows like "Survivor" and "Temptation Island" hold mass appeal precisely because they lay bare cultural assumptions that are usually hidden from public view. The pursuit of power and self-interest is ultimately the bedrock of human reality.

2. With sufficient education, technology, and financial resources, human beings can control the future. For much of human history, life has been "nasty, brutish and short." A few bad harvests could bring hunger and famine. Disease could strike without warning, wiping out entire villages. Marauding bands of warriors appearing out of nowhere could devastate the countryside.

Thankfully, for most people in the West all that has now changed. From about the fifteenth century onward, western society has increasingly assumed that the forces of the natural world, and the structures of society itself, can be tamed and controlled. Our futures are no longer subject to the arbitrary whims of outside influences.

We now can track the changing face of the weather 24 hours a day. Actuary tables, insurance companies, and medical technology have brought statistical precision and the power of science to the ancient mysteries of life and death. Given sufficient analysis and the right combination of public policies and well-trained social workers, every social malady can ultimately be corrected. And we can be certain that wise lawmakers, together with honest law-enforcement officers and a well-trained military, will ensure domestic security at home and the preservation of our national interests abroad. In short, the good news of modernity is that we are in control of the future. Our lives are what we choose to make of them.

3. *Progress in human history can be measured and quantified.* For modern people, the essence of the good life was captured well by a bumper sticker popular in the early 1990s: "He who dies with the most toys wins!" Progress in modern society can be easily measured by indices like a steadily expanding GNP, low inflation, low unemployment, healthy stock markets, and a rising standard of living.

For individuals, progress means that you and your children will have access to more education, more technology, more consumer goods, more leisure, a longer lifespan, and greater freedom to exercise your individual rights than ever before.

God's presence or blessing, if indeed it ever becomes relevant to the conversation, can be calibrated precisely by the number of cars in our garages, credit cards in our wallets, entertainment systems in our homes, and vacations in our future.

4. *First we live . . . and then we die.* Modern people tend to be very inconsistent in their beliefs about life after death. Most Christians, of course, readily affirm—at least in principle—the doctrine of the immortality of the soul. When Christians reflect on their eventual deaths, they are likely to claim that the essence of their identities resides in their souls, not in their physical bodies. And since the soul is immortal and the Bible teaches the promises of heaven, Christians can face death in the confident expectation of an eternal, joyous fellowship with God and all the saints. Ask

any professing Christian about life after death and the chances are very good that you will get some version of this as the right answer.

Yet, oddly enough, when faced with the question of how we would react to an actual threat to our lives, many contemporary Christians offer a response that does not differ in any significant way from what one might expect to hear from a modern non-Christian. That is to say, the preservation of our physical lives—whether our own or that of our loved ones—turns out to be of *ultimate* importance to us. If someone threatens to rob us of our possessions or our lives, then a lethal act of violence against the aggressor is justified. In other words, our own lives must be preserved at all costs even if it means forfeiting the life of someone else, presumably that of a non-Christian.

The conclusion of all this seems to be unavoidably clear. Talk of a soul, or of immortality, or of life after death may provide a psychological boost to help us get through some of the rough spots in life, but in the end many Christians act no differently than their non-Christian neighbors when it comes to using violence to defend our lives against evildoers. This suggests that we actually do fear that life ends with death.

But wait, you may be inclined to argue indignantly, such a view of the world is far too bleak and pessimistic. Certainly we believe in the immortality of the soul. Christians would never reduce human history to a mere struggle for power. Naturally, we believe that God is in control of the universe. Of course it is possible for humans—and, above all, Christians—to act in genuinely unselfish and sacrificial ways. How absurd to think that life is mostly about the security provided by material possessions.

Such a response is undoubtedly made with sincerity and conviction. And yet the troubling reality is that many of us Christians have made our peace with a kind of schizophrenic perspective on God's actual relevance to the world. Our Sunday morning notion of the right answer frequently has no direct bearing on the actual pattern of our behavior during the other six days of the week. If the question is not what we Christians *profess* to believe, but instead how we actually live in the normal world, our behavior frequently points to a perspective that is more Nietzschean than Christian in character.

In its many subtle forms, the Nietzschean worldview is powerful precisely because it seems to conform so well to what we experience in daily life. Pick up any newspaper and you will encounter a host of stories that describe a world driven by power and coercion: public notices of marriage separations and divorce; accounts of ethnic, political, and religious violence; evidence of unjust economic relations, racial divides, broken promises, and misplaced trust. These stories of life's struggles seem to be written into the very nature of reality itself. Thus, a so-called realist simply recognizes that chaos and violence are primordial, as inevitable in history as human selfishness and greed.

At the same time, however, very few people, least of all Christians, are ready to throw up their hands and concede that violence is the only form of power that matters in the world. Throughout history, humans have always sought to restrain or minimize raw expressions of violence in social life. Most people in the U.S., for example, assume that the presence of an armed police force will preserve their personal security at home, while a well-trained standing army, combined with treaties and peace conferences, should be sufficient to defend national interests abroad.

Naturally, we hope that neither the police nor the military will be forced to use lethal violence, but the mere fact that they stand ready to impose order—by force, if necessary—serves to keep our violent impulses in check. Such social restraints on human selfishness have had a largely positive influence in human society. They represent a significant advance over the chaos of anarchy and a world in which only the most violent can survive. Surely it is better that violence be contained than allowed to flourish.

All this may seem obvious enough. And yet from a Christian perspective, such logic deserves a much closer look. In the end, even though police forces and standing armies may preserve social order, they have not ultimately resolved the problem of violence or sufficiently refuted the powerful claims of a Nietzschean worldview. Nor is there anything distinctively Christian about responding to the problem of violence by building more jails or spending more money in military preparedness. Such responses may appeal to our common sense, but they could be promoted just as plausibly by an atheist.

But Aren't Some Wars Just?

Fair enough, you might respond. Maybe there isn't anything *uniquely* Christian about posting a policeman on a street corner or maintaining a well-prepared military force. But historically Christians have indeed addressed the question of violence in human society with an argument that has tried to moderate and restrain the human impulse to resolve differences with violence. Christians throughout history have almost unanimously regarded violence and war as contrary to the teachings of Christ. Very few believers have claimed that the gospels can be used to justify a crusade or holy war.

At the same time, however, Christian theologians since the fifth century have also generally agreed that there are times when Christians might legitimately use lethal violence. Since the intent of these writers is to justify Christian participation in war, the argument is generally known as the Just War theory. In one form or another, explicitly or implicitly, virtually all contemporary Protestant churches, along with the Catholic church, have adopted some version of the Just War theory.

The foundation of Just War arguments can be found in the philosophy of the Roman philosopher Cicero. Writing a century before Christ, Cicero sought to bring a sense of humanitarian balance and restraint to the actions of the Roman army, while still defending his country's powerful military interests. Like most of the Christians who later echoed his arguments, Cicero deplored violence. But he recognized that some measure of violence seemed necessary for the survival of the state, and so he tried to define the conditions under which Roman citizens could legitimately use lethal weapons.

It was the Christian theologian Augustine of Hippo, however, who developed arguments for the Just War in their most sophisticated form. He did so in the context of some very specific circumstances in the history of the early church.

During the early centuries of the church's existence, Christians had suffered sporadic persecution at the hands of various Roman rulers and were widely regarded as a threat to the stability of the Roman state. But early in the fourth century, the persecution of Christians came to a sudden and abrupt end. In 312 A.D., the Roman general Constantine

> *"You just need to look at what the gospel asks, and what war does. The gospel asks that we feed the hungry, give drink to the thirsty, clothe the naked, welcome the homeless, visit the prisoner, and perform works of mercy. War does all the opposite. It makes my neighbor hungry, thirsty, homeless, a prisoner and sick. The gospel asks us to take up our cross. War asks us to lay the cross of suffering on others."*
>
> Dorothy Day

conquered the city of Rome and claimed that the God of Christianity had given him the victory. In the Edict of Milan which he issued the following year, Constantine declared an end to the persecution of Christians and even granted them a favored status within the Roman empire. Suddenly, Christianity went from being an outcast minority point of view to enjoying the blessing of the emperor himself.

This new political framework spared Christians from further persecution. But it also assumed that Christians would now accept responsibility for defending the interests of the empire itself, a new reality that required a reconception of Christian theology.

Augustine's argument defending the principles of a Just War was one important step in this reformulation of Christian thought. Writing about a century after Constantine in the context of a declining Roman empire, Augustine tried to formulate a series of principles that would allow Christians to defend legitimately the boundaries of the empire against barbarian attacks, while also preserving an appropriate sense of restraint and regret when Christians found themselves compelled to use violence against fellow human beings.

The principles were straightforward and fairly simple. For example, according to Augustine Christians could participate in warfare *only if the war had been declared by a proper and legitimate authority.* No Christian was free to use violence in an act of personal vengeance or to raise a private army to pursue some selfish end. Furthermore, Christians could participate in war *only if there was a just cause*—if the country had been attacked by an outside aggressor or if it was going to the aid of a weaker neighbor. Christians could go to war *only if it was a last resort*—if all the standard diplomatic efforts to resolve the conflict had been exhausted. Christians waging war should do so with a *clear sense of moderation and proportion.* They should use the least amount of violence necessary, stopping the war as soon as their objective had been accomplished, and they should *never kill noncombatants.* Finally, Christian soldiers should *kill their enemies with love in their hearts.* Killing another human being should never be done in a passionate rage that dehumanized the enemy, but with great reluctance and regret that higher principles had forced the Christian to take such an action.

From the perspective of Christian pacifists and the historic peace churches, the Just War theory is not entirely bad. It begins appropriately with a recognition that Christ's teachings about loving one's enemy are the ideal and that the need to rationalize a Christian's participation in violence is a clear concession to this higher principle. Moreover, having some stated conditions that restrain or minimize the violence of war is clearly better than a military strategy that has no rules of conduct whatsoever.

Granted all that, however, Just War arguments still leave unresolved a host of questions that discerning Christians must acknowledge before considering this issue settled.

1. Since the time of Augustine the doctrine of the Just War has never prevented a war from breaking out. There are no recorded cases in history in which a nation has chosen *not* to pursue war because the Christians in its government or army made a conscientious decision that a particular conflict did not adequately meet the criteria of a Just War. From the perspective of the nation-state, every war in which it chooses to participate is just.

2. The Just War theory creates the possibility, indeed the probability, that Christians will end up killing each other as combatants on opposite sides of the war, each claiming that their own use of violence can be defended as a genuinely just war. During the first half of the twentieth century, some 50 million Europeans, all of them from ostensibly Christian nations, died killing each other in the battles of World War I and World War II. Inscribed on the belt buckles of the German soldiers in Hitler's army were the words *Gott mit Uns* (God with us), a conviction shared with equal certainty by the Catholic and Protestant soldiers of the Allied forces as each fought to kill the other. Vast cemeteries in the United States and Europe are filled with the gravestones of Christians who were killed by their fellow believers, each claiming to be engaged in a war that somehow fit the criteria of the Just War theory.

3. Very few nations, so-called Christian or otherwise, have actually been willing to limit their military options in accordance with Just War principles, especially if the tide of war begins to turn against them. Even the United States, whose official military policy includes many of the basic principles of the Just War doctrine, has not hesitated to allow expedience to overtake principle if military strategy demanded it. Thus, the firebombing of Dresden or the

atomic bombs dropped on Hiroshima and Nagasaki or the napalm bombing of Vietnam all clearly violate the principle against killing noncombatants.

The Just War doctrine offers a patina of moral decency in times of horrific violence, but, in the end, the conviction that you are fighting for a just cause almost always overrides all other considerations, making it possible to justify virtually any means that will bring about the goal of victory.

4. Finally, and most importantly, there is nothing uniquely Christian about the Just War theory. The foundation of its principles ultimately rest much more firmly on the natural law tradition of Cicero than on the gospel of love taught by Jesus in the New Testament. Its strongest appeal is not to Scripture but to common sense—to an innate notion of justice and the biological urge for self-preservation. In fact, Jesus anticipated this human impulse and addressed it directly. "If you love those who love you, what reward do you have?" Jesus asked plaintively in the middle of his Sermon on the Mount. "Do not even the tax collectors do the same? And if you greet only your brothers and sisters, what more are you doing than others? Do not even the Gentiles do the same?" (Matthew 5:46-47). Christians, Jesus insisted, are called to a higher standard than merely that of natural law, a standard no less than God Himself: "Be perfect, therefore, as your heavenly Father is perfect" (Matthew 5:48).

Modernity's Faith in Reason

Ironically enough, it was precisely the failure of the Just War theory and the stubborn reality of Christian-inspired violence that sparked the emergence of a second major effort in the western tradition to reduce the destructive power of war.

In the course of the sixteenth century, the Protestant Reformation had left European society deeply divided into several competing confessions, each insisting that theirs' was the only true interpretation of scripture and God's will for humanity. Because representatives of each confession—Catholic, Lutheran, Reformed—claimed to be defending divine truth rather than merely the political interests or religious ideas of mortals, all tactics and strategies, no matter how violent, could ultimately be justified if they brought victory. And because God's Truth was at stake in the fighting, surrender to a heretical opponent was unthinkable.

Thus, for more than a century, from the 1520s to 1650, Catholic, Lutheran, and Reformed princes fought each other in a series of bloody and destructive wars, all in defense of their mutually incompatible understandings of Christian faith.

In the context of these seemingly endless religious wars—pitting Christians against Christians—Enlightenment thinkers like Rene Descartes and John Locke came to recognize that religion had become a significant problem for political life. Since Christians reading the same scripture were led by their subjective experiences, prejudices, and superstitions to radically differing interpretations, appeals to religious truth could never be fully resolved and religion could never form a secure basis for a unified nation.

The solution, Enlightenment thinkers claimed, was to ground all discussions about ultimate reality and truth not in religion, but in a secular reality common to all human beings (indeed, inherent in human nature itself): reason. Because reason transcended the particularities of culture, tradition, and religion, it seemed to offer a means of setting aside religious squabbling and providing a truly impartial court of appeal.

With this in mind, political philosophers during the course of the eighteenth century sought to reformulate the foundations of political society on rational, rather than religious, principles. The U.S. Declaration of Independence and Constitution were among the first formal documents to establish a political order based explicitly on reason.

To be sure, religion did not disappear from these documents nor from society altogether. Citizens were free to practice the religion of their choice in these new secular states, and the Founding Fathers did recognize a transcendent Deity as the source of moral law. But debates over specific religious doctrines were to be kept firmly within the bounds of the private sphere. For the first time in western civilization, religion was formally separated from the authority of the state, a model that slowly became the standard for most western nations. In effect, the vexing problem of religious wars in western society was solved by removing religion from political life.

It was only a short step to extend the authority of reason from the world of politics to other areas of society as well. The disciplines of psychology, economics, political science, sociology, and anthropology all emerged in the course of the nineteenth century. Each was confident that reason, combined with the careful research methods of the natural sciences, could lay bare the mysteries of the human psyche and reveal the hidden patterns of economic, political, social, and cultural behavior.

The optimistic hope of these new social sciences was that a systematic and rational approach would solve human problems, especially those related to violence, more effectively than the abstract and contentious claims of religion. When people or nations disagreed and threatened to use violence on each other, the differences could be resolved by an appeal to the most rational argument or the implementation of just the right social design. Confidence in reason and the social sciences remained strong throughout much of the twentieth century. The United Nations came to symbolize the world's hope that a forum for rational discussion of national and regional differences would reduce the threat of war. Summits, conferences, and seminars have sought to bring together the sharpest thinkers from every discipline to debate the merits of various strategies. Billions of dollars have been spent on innumerable studies, trying to uncover the sources of crime, domestic violence, addictions, poverty, and, not surprisingly, war itself. Research centers and think tanks of every imaginable sort have flourished, each committed to the analysis and resolution of some particular social, political, or economic ill.

This modern faith in reason has brought with it some enormous successes. Certain debilitating diseases have been eradicated. We have greatly expanded our capacity to produce large quantities of food. And we have a much better understanding of the sources of violence, both international and domestic, and the necessary conditions for peace and security.

Unfortunately, however, the optimistic hope that reason and the social sciences could resolve the problem of violence in the world has proven to be an illusion. Like the Just War doctrine, modern faith in reason has mitigated some aspects of human violence, but the promise and hope that it offers for peace has far exceeded reality.

In the first place, human experience since the Enlightenment has made it abundantly clear that reason alone cannot prevail over human insecurity and greed.

Long ago, the Greek philosopher Socrates argued that "to know the good, was to will the good." By that he meant that if human beings fully understand what they should do—if they only *know* the good—then, as rational creatures, they will automatically be inclined to actually *do* the right thing.

Only a little bit of reflection, however, makes it clear that Socrates was simply wrong in his confident assessment of the power of reason. All of us know from personal experience that we consistently choose to do things that we know we ought not to do. If, for example, human societies were guided by reason alone, then we would probably recognize that the enormous gap between the richest and the poorest nations of the world contributes to political instability—and those of us in the richest nations would naturally opt for a lower standard of living in the interests of promoting a more just and rational distribution of economic resources. Yet such a policy of voluntarily redistributing money and power is almost certainly not going to gain much ground among American citizens or corporations. Humans simply do not always act rationally.

Further evidence of the failure of the modern confidence in reason can also be found in the bloody history of the twentieth century itself. New applications of reason and the scientific method have not only produced better medicines and improved crop yields, they have also introduced new generations of military weapons with almost unimaginable destructive power. Research laboratories around the world, headed by thoughtful and rational scientists, have created the atomic and hydrogen bombs, new forms of biological and chemical weapons, sophisticated missile systems, sensitive land mines, and a whole arsenal of complex and powerful methods of killing human beings in ever more efficient and effective ways.

Reason and science have clearly not inoculated western culture against violence. Rather, the shadow side of modernity has been a long and bloody history of conquest, enslavement, the Holocaust, and apartheid. Indeed, more people have died violent deaths in the twentieth century than in all of previous human history combined.

Perhaps most disturbing from a Christian perspective is the fact that the modern confidence in reason, like the Just War theory, threatens to make God and Christian faith altogether irrelevant to the realities of daily life. The natural and social sciences have no means of measuring the presence of the Holy Spirit in the laboratory; miracles do not lend themselves well to controlled experiments designed by scientists.

The conclusions for modern people are slowly becoming clear: if ideas or religious truths cannot be apprehended by our physical senses, then they must not exist. Religion, therefore, can be dismissed as an illusion, a culturally created means of coping with the painful stresses and worries of daily life. In the end, material realities in history—class, gender, ethnicity, political interests, etc.—explain the real world much better than religion.

"The Myth of Redemptive Violence"

There is yet a third worldview about the place of violence in human affairs that deserves our attention, an approach that the theologian Walter Wink has helpfully described as the "myth of redemptive violence."[2]

Like the Just War theory, this approach begins with the assumption that violence is a terrible thing, but an inevitable, regretful necessity nevertheless. Like the claims of reason, the myth of redemptive violence offers itself as a pragmatic strategy, rooted in our deep-seated notions of fairness and justice. But it differs from these other two approaches in that it is not a propositional doctrine (like the Just War theory) or a historically conditioned way of thinking (like the modern faith in reason). Though it shares many features of both, it is more primal than these approaches, more deeply grounded in our most basic understandings of reality, and thus more powerful in shaping our worldview and our actions.

The identity of virtually every civilization or culture, claims Wink, is rooted in a primal creation story about its beginning. These stories, or myths, provide a narrative account of the earliest history of the group, but they also establish a moral structure for the group's deepest, most enduring, values. They distill the essence of a group's assumptions about human nature, about how humans relate to each other, and the ways in which humans interact with the divine.

While the details of these creation stories differ widely across time and space, they very frequently share a basic structure or plotline. Most stories begin with an account of a battle between the forces of evil (the Other) and the forces of good (Us). Often the odds are stacked heavily in favor of the forces of evil since evildoers do not hesitate to use tactics of cheating, lying, duplicity, and brute violence. By contrast, our own deepest qualities are rooted in the civilizing principles of goodness, decency, honesty, love, and compassion.

At some point in this battle—usually just as the forces of evil are about to prevail—the powers of good find themselves compelled, against their wishes, to respond to evil with a brutal violence of their own, descending to the level of the evildoers themselves. But this is a righteous vio-

> *"Our wagon fortress is Christ, our weapon of defense is patience. Our sword is the Word of God and our victory is free, firm and undisguised faith in Christ Jesus. Iron, metal, spears and swords we leave to those who (alas) consider men's and pigs' blood of about the same worth!"*
>
> Menno Simons, 1539

lence, a *redemptive* violence, that is swift and furious in its focus and outcome. It is a violence absolutely necessary if goodness is going to prevail against the forces of evil. And once it has accomplished its purpose, it is quickly set aside in favor of the more civilized ideals of justice and truth.

Such a story line is a foundational premise of modern life. Indeed, claims Wink, the dominant religion in our society today is not Judaism or Christianity or Islam, but the myth of redemptive violence.[3] Such an assertion may sound like an exaggeration until you start to look for elements of this basic plotline and discover it appearing virtually everywhere.

The myth of redemptive violence, for example, has provided the rationale for every war in the political history of the United States (the Revolutionary War, the Civil War, the world wars of the twentieth century, and the most recent war on terrorism). It is the subplot of virtually all martial arts and action movies and most Saturday morning cartoons. It is the iron law of the Western, where a lone gunman, usually seeking nothing more than to be left alone in peace and tranquility, finds himself defending the lives of innocent settlers by finally turning (but always as a last resort, only after every peaceful means of resolving the conflict has been exhausted) to violence. In every instance the violence is redemptive in nature. Goodness is defended against evil; civility and order are restored; and peace is the inevitable outcome.

The myth of redemptive violence is so powerful both because it reveals our most basic assumptions about the nature of reality and because it usually operates at a deeply subconscious level. Consider, for example, the popular Steven Spielberg movie "Saving Private Ryan," released to great public and critical acclaim in 1998. The main focus of the story turns on the efforts of Captain John Miller (Tom Hanks) and his handpicked team of ordinary citizen soldiers to rescue James Ryan, the one surviving son of a grieving mother whose three other boys have already died in combat.

From one perspective, "Saving Private Ryan" is deeply ambiguous about the nature of violence. Like many standard war movies, it begins with dramatic scenes of sacrifice and heroism (the storming of Omaha Beach), and it ends with more scenes of sacrifice and heroism (the defense of the bridge at Cherbourg, the death of Captain Miller, and the "saving" of Private Ryan).

But these battle scenes are so horrific and gruesome in their depiction of the ugliness of war, that no typical viewer would leave the theater inspired to sign up at the nearest military recruiting station. Moreover, Spielberg does not shrink back from the many moral ambiguities of the battlefield, especially the dubious logic of sacrificing the lives of seven men in order to bring a single soldier home alive. In many ways the movie raises a series of haunting questions about the folly of war and its dehumanizing impact on everyone who participates in it. "Saving Private Ryan" is not a simplistic or formulaic remake of the standard war movies that glorify gratuitous violence.

At the same time, however, in a much more subtle and powerful way, a crucial subplot of "Saving Private Ryan" unfolds that dramatically embraces the ancient cultural myth of redemptive violence. The main character in this subplot is not Captain Miller or the six soldiers he has handpicked to serve on the mission; rather the hero in the myth of redemptive violence turns out to be a newcomer to the team—Corporal Timothy Upham, a translator who is proficient in French and German but has never seen combat duty or fired a gun at another human being.

In a crucial scene early in their search for Private Ryan, the group stumbles into a German ambush and a fierce gunfight ensues, resulting in the gruesome, agonizing death of a young American soldier. Miller's team captures the only surviving German, the man likely responsible for the young American's death. Incensed by the loss of their comrade, the group forces the German soldier to dig his own grave and prepares to execute him.

But then the tide suddenly turns. Corporal Upham, the translator, converses with the soldier in German, recognizes in him a fellow human being, and begs that his life be spared. Against the strong wishes of the team, hungry for vengeance, Captain Miller agrees with Upham.

What follows is a surprising moment of forgiveness (the disarmed German soldier is set free) and of self-revelation (the team discovers that Captain Miller, this battle-hardened hero of Omaha Beach, was formerly a high school English teacher in a small town in Pennsylvania). "The more men I kill," Miller tells his troops in defense of his decision, "the further away from home I feel."

The moral message is clear: to kill an unarmed person, even a soldier in uniform who has just shot your comrade, is beyond the bounds of civilized conduct. Amid the horrifying violence of war, forgiveness and compassion keep us tethered to our very humanity. But in true Nietzschean fashion, no good deed goes unpunished. This act of kindness, this expression of pacifist charity, soon comes back to haunt the Americans. At the end of the climactic battle scene we discover that this same freed soldier reappears once again, rifle in hand, among the Germans attacking the bridge Miller and his troops are now defending. And in the end, it is this very soldier, this recipient of grace and forgiveness, who takes aim and, without shame or remorse, kills Captain Miller, the man who only days before had spared his life. Now it is Corporal Upham's turn to take center stage.

Upham, the gentle translator who abhors violence of every sort, suddenly finds himself face to face with the German soldier who is now a disarmed prisoner of war. Here is the real moment of truth, the moral hinge upon which the movie turns. Will Upham, in a compassionate, New-Testament spirit of "seventy times seven forgiveness," again recognize the common bond of humanity he shares with the enemy—whom we see once more begging for mercy—and spare the life of this evil person? The choice is his.

Yet for those attuned to the myth of redemptive violence such an outcome is no longer thinkable. Such behavior would be too unrealistic. And so, true to the demands of common sense and the cultural plotline, Upham resolves his moral dilemma by taking careful aim at the German soldier and shooting him dead. In so doing, the unjust death of Captain Miller and the rest of his team is vindicated. The limits of principled restraint and pacifism are clearly demonstrated and a deeper truth revealed: violence, under extreme circumstances, is redemptive.

Even more than the formal ethical theory of the Just War or the modern faith in reason, the myth of redemptive violence has a seductive power that blinds us to its real consequences. One crucial element of the myth is the illusion that a justified use of violence will somehow conclusively resolve the problem of evil, bringing a decisive end to the escalating cycle of destruction that gave rise to the confrontation in the first place.

Yet despite our deepest hopes to the contrary, the truth of the matter is that violence—no matter how redemptive its claims—inevitably begets more violence. Wars "to end all wars" turn out to be vain illusions; "final solutions" have horrific legacies; campaigns to eradicate terrorists invariably sow the seeds of still more vindictive terrorism in the future.

The myth of redemptive violence also assumes that my cause is not only righteous, but that it is worth more than your life—my redemption comes at the price of your death. As the bloody conflicts between Protestants and Catholics in Ireland or Palestinians and Israelis in the West Bank or Tutsis and Hutus in Rwanda have made clear, opposing sides can be equally certain about the righteousness of their cause. And all too frequently, it is precisely the claims to righteousness, deeply woven into the collective consciousness, that make these conflicts so bitter and prolonged.

In the end, redemptive violence is a myth for Christians because there is nothing Christian about its logic. If every human being is indeed made in the very image of God, then what argument can possibly justify one of God's creatures—especially one who has come to know and claim the love of God—to take the life of another human?

Conclusion

All of these responses to violence—the Just War, reason, and redemptive violence—have in their favor the powerful logic of common sense. Each of them resorts to violence only reluctantly, always in defense of some higher principle that dare not be sacrificed to the brute force of tyranny. Each seeks to defend, sacrificially if necessary, innocent people against unwarranted suffering. Yet all of these attempts to mitigate violence in human society also reinforce the Nietzschean assumption that ultimately the universe is defined most fundamentally by coercion and violence.

It may be natural for us to justify our use of violence and to distinguish righteous violence from evil violence. But such efforts cannot hide the fact that violence is the common denominator of our definitions of both good and evil. All of these approaches end up suggesting that God's presence in the universe blesses *our* violence against the violence of the aggressor, so that it is not God, but we, who are finally in control of history.

The haunting question remains. On the question of violence, do Christians have anything *different* to offer the world than strategies that are ultimately based on power and coercion? If not, is their worldview any different in principle than a Nietzschean perspective in which God is as good as dead?

Where in the midst of this can we find a gospel that is genuinely good news?

---

[1] Nietzsche, *The Gay Science* (New York: Vintage Books, 1974), pp. 182ff.

[2] Walter Wink, *The Powers That Be: Theology for a New Millennium* (New York: Doubleday, 1998), 42-62.

[3] Ibid., 42.

3.

THE GOOD NEWS
OF THE GOSPEL
OF PEACE

*"It is hard to make your adversaries real people unless
you recognize yourself in them—in which case, if you
don't watch out, they cease to be adversaries."*

Flannery O'Connor,
The Habit of Being: Letters of Flannery O'Connor

In the aftermath of apartheid's collapse in South Africa in
1994, the new government under Nelson Mandela established a Truth and Reconciliation Commission whose
task it was to investigate specific acts of brutality committed
in the name of apartheid and to seek some measure of resolution that would enable the country to move forward.

At one meeting early in their work, the commission gathered to reach a verdict on a particularly painful case involv-
ing an elderly South African woman. At the hearing, a group
of white police officers, led by a Mr. Van de Broek, admitted
their personal responsibility in the death of her 18-year-old
son. They acknowledged shooting the young man at point-
blank range, setting his body on fire, and then partying
around the fire until the body had been reduced to little

more than ashes. Eight years later, van de Broek and his fellow officers had again intersected with the woman's life, this time to take her husband into captivity. And then, some time later, van de Broek had come knocking at her door once more. Rousing her from bed in the dead of night, he brought the woman to an isolated setting by a river where her husband lay tied to a pile of wood. As she watched, he and the officers doused the man with gasoline and then ignited a fire. The last words her husband spoke to her, in the midst of the blazing pyre, were "Forgive them."

Now at long last the time had come for justice to be served. Those involved had confessed their guilt, and the Commission turned to the woman for a final statement regarding her desire for an appropriate punishment.

"I want three things," the woman said calmly. "I want Mr. van de Broek to take me to the place where they burned my husband's body. I would like to gather up the dust and give him a decent burial.

"Second, Mr. van de Broek took all my family away from me and I still have a lot of love to give. Twice a month, I would like for him to come to the ghetto and spend a day with me so I can be a mother to him.

"Third, I would like Mr. van de Broek to know that he is forgiven by God, and that I forgive him, too. And, I would like someone to come and lead me by the hand to where Mr. van de Broek is so that I can embrace him and he can know my forgiveness is real."

As the elderly woman made her way across the silent courtroom, van de Broek reportedly fainted, overcome by emotion. And then the silence was broken when someone began singing "Amazing Grace." Others soon picked up the words of the familiar hymn, so that finally the entire audience in the courtroom was joined in song.[1]

The point of this chapter is captured—precisely and elo- quently—in the drama that unfolded that day before the Truth and Reconciliation Commission. The harmony God intended for us in creation has been shattered by sin. We live in a world filled with alienation and violence—a world that too frequently reduces human beings, created in God's image, to ashes. But Christians can testify to the fact that this is not the end of the story. Throughout history God has persistently and sacrificially invited humans back to the wholeness and fellowship for which they were cre- ated. Even while we were His enemies, God offered us His love and forgiveness, making possible our redemption through the compassionate life, the sacrificial death, and joyous resurrection of His son, Jesus Christ.

According to the witness of the apostles and the New Testament church, this good news of salvation is only the beginning of the story, not its ending. For just as God has freely extended His love to us, so too we are called to reach out with this same spirit of generosity and forgiveness to others, including, as in the case of the elderly South African woman, those who might be regarded as our enemies.

For centuries, the mainstream body of Christian believ- ers, Catholic and Protestant alike, have regarded the gospel of peace as a high calling for the heroic individual, or a description of heavenly perfection, or as the eccentric teaching of a few radical sectarian groups—but not as a principle central to the gospel itself. In this chapter I want to suggest that reconciliation with our enemies is not merely a part of the good news of the gospel we have received, it *is* the gospel—the very heart of our faith which Christians are called to embody in their daily lives and to share freely with all those who are not yet in fellowship with God.

Created for Shalom . . .

To understand the centrality of nonviolent love to the Christian gospel we must start by looking again at the biblical story of creation where we find crucial clues into God's original intentions for humanity and for creation itself. The first chapter of Genesis describes a God who appeared out of nowhere, created being out of nothingness, and brought order out of chaos. In contrast to the creation stories of many other Middle Eastern peoples, there is no hint in Genesis of a grand cosmic battle in which God needed to defeat other rivals in order for creation to come into being. The biblical account of creation does not rest on a primal, violent struggle for power. Rather, God simply called creation into being with a series of commands: first light was separated from darkness; then the heavens were separated from the earth and the seas from dry land. Then, after calling forth creatures of every imaginable sort to inhabit the sea and the air and the earth, God shaped the first human being "in His own image and likeness" and made that clay form come alive with the power of His own life-giving breath.

Significantly, the biblical account is emphatic that all of creation radiated with God's blessing and benediction: "God saw everything that He had made, and indeed, it was very good" (Genesis 1:31). Unlike the Nietzschean worldview, which assumes that reality at its core is embattled and chaotic, the story told in Genesis begins with a description of an ordered and peaceful creation, one called into being out of nothing and pronounced by the Creator of the universe to be "good."

The verses that follow the story of creation sketch the outline of a world that is in balance and at peace. Made in God's very image, Adam and Eve were created for the purpose of friendship and fellowship with God. Flesh of each other's flesh, they were also designed to live with each other in complete intimacy and trust. Surrounded by the lush verdancy of a garden, they were intended to live in balance with the natural world around them. The Hebrew word for this original state of affairs, *Shalom*, describes well the all-encompassing harmony of creation's original design.

This is how we were meant to live. God created us to be citizens of Eden: to walk in fellowship with Him in the coolness of the morning, to live in peace with every other human being, to celebrate the wonders and bountiful riches of nature. We were created for this Shalom. Our yearnings

> "*Christ made peace with all our enemies, too, on the cross. Let us bear witness to this peace to all.*"
>
> Dietrich Bonhoeffer,
> *A Testament to Freedom*

for spiritual communion with God, the deep longings we have for intimacy with each other, our sense of wonder in the face of nature's beauty—all of this is a profound reminder of our intended purpose in creation.

. . . Distorted by Sin

And yet the very notions of *yearning* and *longing* already hint at the fact that something in God's intended purpose for humanity has gone badly wrong. The story of the Fall, coming in Genesis 3 almost before the bare outlines of life in Eden have even been sketched, reminds us that our hunger for Shalom—our deep desire for trust and communion with God and with each other—has been poisoned by sin. Against God's expressed command, Adam and Eve succumbed to the temptation to "be as God" by grasping the fruit of the tree of knowledge of good and evil.

With that act, everything changed. Like Adam and Eve, we are now conscious of ourselves as free moral agents, capable of distinguishing between good and evil, faced with genuine choices, and free to choose in matters of life and death.

That freedom, however, came at the cost of a deep disruption to the original Shalom of creation. As described in Genesis, when God came to walk with them in the coolness of the garden, Adam and Eve, now empowered with moral discernment, recognized with appropriate shame just how far short they had fallen from God's righteousness. Embarrassed, they tried to hide. Similarly, Adam and Eve suddenly became aware of their own nakedness and vulnerability to each other, and so they fashioned clothes to mask their true selves. Expelled from the Garden, Adam and Eve found themselves living "east of Eden," engaged in a fierce struggle with nature for their very survival.

Perhaps the most dramatic evidence that Shalom had been shattered is an account of humankind's first act of violence. Driven by jealousy and pride, Cain killed his brother Abel, and for this deed he was forced into exile as an eternal wanderer—an apt metaphor of the human condition ever since.

In the movie "Grand Canyon," the main character—a wealthy accountant—finds himself stalled, late at night, in a rough section of town. While the tow truck is on its way, five young gang members surround the car and begin to threaten the terrified man. When the tow truck arrives, the driver quickly realizes what is happening. Streetwise himself, he takes the gang leader aside and makes an exasperated plea for them to move on without doing any harm. "Man," he says, "the world ain't supposed to work like this. Maybe you don't know that, but this ain't the way it's supposed to be. I'm supposed to do my job without asking you if I can. That dude is supposed to be able to wait with his car without you ripping him off. *Everything is supposed to be different than the way it is here.*"

The tow-truck driver's statement captures our experience of the world exactly. Made in the image of God, breathing God's very breath of life, human beings carry within themselves an indelible memory of God's original intention and design. Somewhere deep in our hearts we know that we are intended to live in fellowship with God and in harmony with each other. Yet all around and within us are persistent reminders that we are alienated from our true design, exiles and refugees from our intended homeland. The way the world is is not the way it is supposed to be.

If this were the end of the story, then the Bible would be a brief book indeed. But remarkably, against all odds, the creation account does not end with the Fall or with the Flood. Instead, it resumes again, shaped now by God's persistent, loving invitations for humans to return to the Shalom for which they were originally intended.

As we all know, creation remains out of joint. The full restoration of the Garden of Eden must await the end of time with the gathering of the saints at the great Wedding Banquet of the Lamb. But until then, all of Scripture and the entire history of the Christian church relate an amazing story of God's creative initiative in extending the gift of Shalom to all those who are willing to trust Him.

Covenant, Law and Kingship: Shalom Recovered?

The restoration of Shalom unfolds slowly and hesitatingly. The Old Testament narrative is filled with accounts both of God's repeated initiatives for reconciliation and the tortuous refrain of human faithlessness and apostasy.

Woven into that many-layered story, however, are three significant themes, each of which offers a clear insight into the nature of God's character and God's ongoing, creative presence in human history.

Covenant—trust yields a blessing

One of the first tangible signs that God has not given up on the ideal of Shalom comes in the story of Abram as told in Genesis 12. We know very little about Abram before his surprising encounter with God. He was apparently a wealthy person, living a life of comfort and ease in the territory of Ur. Then, according to the biblical account, God interrupted his secure life and offered to make an agreement or a Covenant with him. The Covenant, initiated by God, had conditions that each party promised to fulfill: if Abram would agree to trust God fully and completely—if he were to pack his bags, gather his family and servants, and launch out on a trek to some unknown destination—then God would guarantee him innumerable descendants and would make Abram's people into a great and mighty nation.

Abram agreed to this "mutually exclusive partnership." He resettled from Ur to Canaan, changed his name to Abraham to reflect his new identity, and, with his aging wife Sarah, became parents of a miracle child who ensured the continuity of his lineage.

This simple Covenant between God and Abraham became the foundation of a new ethnic and religious group—the Hebrew people, or the Children of Israel—and a whole new worldview. It solidified the character of God as a "jealous" God who expects complete trust and obedience from His people in return for His blessing. This is a God who actively maintains his part of the Covenant, intervening miraculously in the lives of Abraham's descendants. This is a God who defends His people when they are weak and powerless, a God who chastises and punishes His people when they disobey.

At key moments in their history, the Hebrew people reaffirmed the Covenant made with Abraham by renewing their commitment to put their trust in God alone or by reciting the stories of how God's "mighty hand and outstretched arm" had saved them from their enemies. The Covenant thus emerges as a central theme in the Old Testament, a reminder of God's active initiative in human history and the blessings that come when God's people put their trust completely in Him.

Law—A framework for Shalom

A second echo of Shalom resounding throughout the Old Testament came, again at God's initiative, at another crucial moment in the history of the Hebrew people. After a long period of enslavement under the Egyptian pharaohs, Moses led the Children of Israel in a dramatic escape out of Egypt into the Sinai peninsula, following God's promise to grant them a land of their own. As former slaves in an oppressive culture, the Hebrew people had had little experience in self-government, and they found themselves wandering in uncharted territory, uncertain about their future survival.

Yet once again God intervened in a decisive way, this time by establishing a clear code of behavior—the Ten Commandments—which became the basis for a more detailed set of principles known as the Law (or Torah).

Modern people are inclined to think of the Law in rather negative terms: as a restriction on our freedoms or an imposed narrowing of our choices. Yet without law, a community quickly descends into anarchy. Without law, justice is inevitably defined and imposed by the mighty. Without law, those in power can easily become tyrannical.

In the Amish community near my home, each congregation or district is united by something the Amish call the *Ordnung*. The Ordnung is a set of basic understandings, most of them unwritten, that literally gives "order" to the communal life of these earnest Christians. The Ordnung addresses a wide variety of activities regulating acceptable Amish practice in such areas as dress, education, technology, communication, and transportation. To the outsider looking in, the Ordnung can often seem to be legalistic and oppressive—a clear infringement on individual freedoms.

Yet millions of tourists flock each year to visit Amish communities. And the source of that attraction is nearly always rooted in a fascination with the structure and discipline of their lives. Without the Ordnung, there would be no Amish. In the words of essayist Wendell Berry, the Amish "have mastered one of the fundamental paradoxes of our condition: we can make ourselves whole only by accepting our partiality, by living within our limits, by being human—not be trying to be gods. By restraint they make themselves whole."

This is the vision of the Law in the biblical tradition. Obedience to the Law not only demonstrated faithfulness and trust in God, but it also brought the blessing of a community that was rooted in justice and committed to the well-being of each individual. Rather than being oppressive, the Law was a gift of God reflecting His love and compassion, a signpost pointing the Hebrew people toward the Shalom of an ordered, fair, and just community.

Godly Kings—the union of justice and might
A third symbol of God's ongoing effort to invite humanity back to the Shalom for which they were intended can be seen in the unique character of political leadership in the Old Testament.

Initially, Israel's demand that God give them a king— "so that we may be like other nations" (I Samuel 8:20)— seemed to mark a step away from the ideal of complete dependence on God alone. But when Israel eventually received a king, the power granted the monarch was pointedly restrained by an even higher moral authority claimed by the prophets.

Every society faces the enduring challenge of balancing the coercive power necessary to preserve social order with the demands of justice that protect the weak and keep political power from descending into tyranny. In Book I of Thomas More's famous *Utopia*, the narrator, a counselor to the king, describes his frustration in trying to bring human law in line with the law of God. Imagine, he says, if in a gathering of generals discussing war strategy he would admonish the king to "let other kingdoms alone, since his own is big enough"; or if, in a conference of experts seeking ways to extract new taxes from the people, he would tell the king to "live on his own income without wronging others, and limit his expenses to his revenue." In either case, claims the narrator, he would be thrown out of the room or regarded as a fool. The problem, as he goes on to explain, is the apparent incompatibility of "might" and "right": might without right leads inevitably to tyranny; yet right without might is powerless to accomplish anything. For Thomas More, the way out of the conundrum was to imagine a distant land—a "utopia" (literally: "no place")—where the exercise of reason would enable the rulers to find just the right balance between order and justice.

But the Old Testament suggests that this ideal can actually be realized in historical time and space. The model of political leadership that emerged within the Jewish community is that of a king who was *both* mighty and righteous, a king whose authority resided not only in the power of his armies but in the fairness of his law. To be sure, the Old Testament account is also filled with examples of ungodly kings who ignored God's commandments and simply sought power for their own sakes. But the ideal of political leadership is clear, epitomized in the example of King David.

Like most biblical heroes, David was not perfect. In fact, he once was so filled with lust for another man's wife that he arranged to have her husband murdered so that he could take her for himself (2 Samuel 11). But Israel's king David steadfastly sought to rule with justice, to honor the Law, and to submit himself to God's higher authority. When the prophet Nathan confronted him about his adultery and murder, David immediately and publicly expressed contrition (2 Samuel 12). The story of David's abuse of power thus underscores the larger point that the authority of a godly king is always restrained by a higher moral law.

As a model king, David stands in sharp contrast to many other biblical rulers who ignored the prophets and God's Law, put their faith in chariots of iron, and chose to do what was right in their own eyes. The ideal he established of a king who united political order with divine justice illustrates, no less than the Covenant and the Law, God's ongoing efforts to call His people back to the Shalom for which they were intended.

Jubilee and the True Spirit of the Law

These Old Testament themes of Shalom—God's Covenant with Abraham's descendants, the gift of the Law, and the ideal of a godly king—all point in the direction of the harmonious relationships that God desires for all of humanity. But they clearly were only a beginning step. Covenant, Law and godly kings could provide a basic framework for human flourishing, but they still fell short of the full ideal suggested in Genesis 1-3.

For an even deeper understanding of Shalom, we need to look carefully at a series of additional hints provided in the Old Testament literature, especially in the books of the prophets. The practice of "Jubilee" described in Deuteronomy 15 and Leviticus 25 offered yet another concrete means of bringing the community even closer to the Shalom God intended for His people. According to the principle of Jubilee, the Hebrew community was to engage in a periodic and systematic leveling of economic relationships. Every seven years all debts were to be forgiven, all indentured servants were allowed to go free, and the farmland was to be left fallow. On a 50-year cycle, all land was to be restored to its original owners.

Scholars are uncertain as to whether or not the Jewish community actually put these ideals into practice. But the basic message is unmistakably clear: put your trust *fully* in God, not in material possessions; treat each other with dignity; build your community on the principles of compassion and generosity. In the vision of Jubilee we see a model for the restoration of Shalom that seems to fly in the face of common sense and conventional wisdom.

Jacob Shenk was a Christian businessman living in Virginia in the 1930s and '40s. A far-sighted entrepreneur, he had established a thriving hatchery business supplying fertilized eggs and grain to local farmers who raised chickens which he, in turn, processed and sold. Shenk simply assumed that his Christian convictions would shape his business, even though many of his practices seemed to defy basic economic logic.

Early in his career, for example, in the spirit of Old Testament Jubilee, he resolved to give away 90% of all his profits to charitable causes. Only after repeatedly auditing his books, did the IRS finally become convinced that this was not a scam. Once, when Shenk had had a particularly good year, he divided some of the unexpected profits among all of the people who had supplied him with eggs. When one of the surprised recipients of this generosity

> *"Though justice be thy plea, consider this:*
> *That in the course of justice none of us*
> *Should see salvation. We do pray for mercy,*
> *And that same prayer doth teach us all to render*
> *The deeds of mercy."*
> **William Shakespeare**

returned the check saying that he had not done anything to deserve it, Shenk simply reissued the check, with a terse note: "company policy, period." When he died in a plane crash in 1950, his non-Christian business associates testified at the funeral that they had never before encountered the likes of Jacob Shenk.

This notion that true Shalom goes beyond merely a formal covenant or keeping the letter of the law finds further expression throughout the entire Old Testament. The prophet Amos repeatedly thundered to his listeners that

God cares more about concrete acts of mercy—especially to the poor and fatherless—than He does about the ritual requirements of worship (Amos 5:21-24).

The same theme echoed in Micah's insistence that the only true requirement of God's people is that they are to "do justice, and to love kindness, and to walk humbly with God" (Micah 6:8). And the point is unmistakably evident in the many prophetic teachings, especially those in Isaiah, that look forward expectantly to a fuller revelation of God's presence and purpose in the form of a Messiah (Isaiah 9:7; 42:1-4; 52:13; 53:9).

The writings of the prophets thus offer persistent reminders that the true fullness of Shalom intended by God still awaited its culmination.

Political Despair . . . and Hopes for a Messiah

As the Old Testament drew to a close, Abraham's descendants are still searching for a Shalom that always seems to elude their grasp. Following the powerful rule of David and his son Solomon, for example, many of Israel's later kings proved to be unfaithful to the Covenant and quickly adopted the gods of neighboring cultures.

In time, 10 of the original 12 tribes of Israel disappeared from history altogether, swallowed up by more powerful invading peoples. The two remaining tribes suffered a long period of conquest and exile under the Babylonians. The glory of the old Covenant and Law, along with the ideal of a godly king, had gradually become a fading memory, preserved in the stories of the past more than in the living reality of the present. In 198 B.C. the Syrians conquered Jerusalem and despoiled the temple by sacrificing a pig, a ritually unclean animal, on the altar. Though the Jewish people eventually reclaimed the city and cleansed the temple, they were overwhelmed once again in 63 B.C. by a new and even more powerful civilization, the Romans.

The Romans ruled Israel with an iron hand, especially after 6 A.D. when Judea became a province with a governor who served directly under the authority of the Emperor. Pilate, who eventually presided over Jesus' crucifixion, was a particularly brutal ruler whose administration was marked by high taxes, widespread corruption, and general brutality.

Thus, at the time of Jesus' birth, Shalom seemed like a distant dream indeed for the Jewish community. Living under the heavy-handed rule of a foreign power, they were a tiny, virtually insignificant people, dwarfed by some of the most powerful military states history had ever known. Yet at the same time, their scriptures preserved memories of bygone glory and, against all odds, fueled fervent hopes that a Messiah—an Anointed One, long promised by the prophets—would come to liberate them from foreign oppression and usher in a new age worthy of Israel's former glory.

At the same time, however, the Jewish community found itself deeply divided over the exact form that liberating Messiah would take. At one extreme were the Zealots, an underground Jewish militia group who had mounted a stubborn, largely unsuccessful, guerilla campaign to evict the Romans from the territory. The Zealots preached a form of holy violence in which they regarded the killing of the godless as a form of religious duty.

At the opposite extreme were the well-to-do Sadduccees. These religious conservatives were eager to accommodate the Roman authorities, even if it meant adapting new religious teachings and practices, as long as they did not interfere with their business arrangements or privileged status.

Somewhere in between, the Pharisees emerged as a reform party advocating the rigorous observance of Old Testament Law as an expression of faithfulness and renewal. And at the very edges of Jewish society were the Essenes, a sectarian monastic-like group that retreated from all worldly affairs, Jewish and Roman alike, to their isolated disciplined communities in the desert.

Each of these groups, in very different ways, offered an alternative path to the future for a community desperately in need of Shalom. Each group claimed to speak in the name of God, arguing its case on the basis of Scripture. Each understood itself to be a faithful embodiment of the Covenant and the Law. Each had reason to hope that the long-awaited Messiah would take up its cause and restore Israel to its former glory.

Shalom Revealed: The Message and Meaning of Christ

When Jesus burst on the scene in first century Palestine he confused and surprised them all.

To be sure, the message he brought to his contemporaries was familiar, clearly rooted in the central themes of the Old Testament. The Scriptures he quoted, the language he spoke, the images that mattered most to him, all came directly out of the well-known accounts of God acting in the history of Abraham and his descendants.

Yet at the same time, his message was fresh and new and unexpected. So much so, in fact, that his followers would later testify that in Christ, creation itself effectively began anew—not only in the calendar sense of time being recalculated by the date of his birth, but also in the more profound reality of the restoration of Shalom to a fallen and sinful humanity. "For as all die in Adam," wrote the apostle Paul, "so all will be made alive in Christ" (1 Corinthians 15:22). Or, again: "So if anyone is in Christ, there is a new creation: everything old has passed away; see, everything has become new" (2 Corinthians. 5:17).

In some ways the fresh, history-transforming excitement of the coming of Christ has been dulled by our over-familiarity with the story of his life. Our tendency to talk about faith primarily in terms of a *personal* relationship makes it easy to reduce Jesus to a vague bundle of feelings, a warm ideal of Love, or, worse, a projection of our own needs and desires. In our imaginations, Jesus is often frozen in a pose fixed by popular paintings: as a gentle shepherd, or a man knocking on a large wooden door, or a kind face gazing up into the light as in a high school graduation photo.

In the Christian church year, Jesus frequently gets locked into his miraculous birth at Christmas or the story of his death and resurrection at Easter. These events, of course, are all crucial to Christian faith. Jesus' birth, death, and resurrection are all historical facts; they are essential to his character and mission. But we can easily adopt a very truncated version of the gospel if we focus so much on his birth and death that we skip over the central message of his teaching. Like the splintered Jewish community of first-century Palestine, modern believers can become so certain about the form their version of Christianity must take, that they miss out on the energy of Jesus' teachings with its power to "make all things new."

The good news of the gospel is that Christ offers humans not only the means of a new relationship with God in a spiritual sense. His life and teachings also provide a road map for how we humans are to live in relationship with other people in our daily lives. In the concrete details of his life, Jesus consciously drew on the Old Testament themes of Covenant, Law, kingship, and Jubilee and transformed them into historical possibilities. As we follow the example of Christ in our daily lives, salvation takes on a tangible expression, and discipleship becomes the path to a deep sense of joy and purpose.

Repent!

When Jesus began his ministry as an itinerant preacher in the countryside of Galilee, people found him interesting—and offensive—in part because he told them they needed to repent. In his gospel account, Matthew reports that almost from the moment of his baptism Jesus began to call on his listeners to "repent, for the kingdom of heaven has come near" (Matthew 4:17). In Luke, Jesus described his mission as calling "sinners to repentance" (Luke 5:32). And in the gospel of Mark, Jesus' disciples took up the same theme when he sent them out, two by two, to preach "that all should repent" (Mark 6:12).

We tend to think of repentance in the emotional sense of remorse or regret or sorrow for our sins. But Jesus had something even more profound in mind in his use of the term. For him, repentance (*metanoia*, in the Greek) meant a new understanding of reality—a transformation of perspective, a new worldview, a fundamentally fresh way of looking at life itself that was at odds with natural or commonly held perspectives on the world. When Jesus called his listeners to repent, he was telling them to change their way of thinking and living. Turn around! Reorient yourselves! Head in a new direction! Align yourselves with the new kingdom that is now being initiated—a new movement of God's presence.

Millard Fuller, founder and director of Habitat for Humanity, describes the beginnings of this remarkable ministry in the New Testament language of "repentence."

From the time he was a college student, Fuller had an amazing knack for making money. Every enterprise he started, it seemed, turned a profit, so that before the age of 30 he was a millionaire with a fancy house, a family, and all of the trappings of the good life. But when his personal life began to collapse and his marriage teetered on the edge of divorce, Fuller realized that something drastic needed to change in his life. Responding to a clear sense of God's calling, he and his wife agreed to sell their business and all of their assets, give the money away, and start over.

In the years that followed, Fuller became the catalyst for one of the most effective Christian ministries of recent history. Enlisting the energies of volunteer labor and local donations, Habitat for Humanity has provided thousands of families in North America and around the world with affordable housing. "I didn't go into Habitat because I love housing," Fuller says, "My passion was to be a witness for Jesus in the world, and this is my way of doing it." Today, Habitat has some 2,000 affiliates and has constructed more than 120,000 homes. Yet it all started with a decision to "turn around."

On this point, the message of the New Testament is clear: the restoration of Shalom, the possibility of a "new creation," begins with repentance.

Be restored to wholeness!

If the path to Shalom began with repentance, the outlines of the restoration it brings were found in the acts of healing that came to define Jesus' ministry. One aspect of the healings recorded in the gospels was symbolic. The calling of the 12 disciples, for example, whose lives represented the full diversity of the Jewish people, marked the restoration, or healing, of the 12 tribes of Israel who were scattered and in disarray.

In a similar fashion, Jesus' calming of the storm signaled to his followers that those who trusted fully in God could live at peace with the forces of nature rather than in fear. Jesus' reference to God as "Abba" (or "Daddy"), underscored a new kind of intimacy that believers can enjoy with the Creator of the universe.

But beyond these symbolic forms of reconciliation, Jesus' ministry of healing very often took on more concrete and tangible forms. Wherever he went, Jesus restored people to *physical* wholeness. The blind received sight, the lame walked again, the deaf could hear, the dead were raised back to life. Wherever he went, Jesus restored people to *emotional* wholeness, offering words of blunt honesty and forgiveness to the woman at the well (John 4:4-30) or a message of reconciliation in the story of the Prodigal Son (Luke 15:11-32). And wherever he went, Jesus restored people to a *spiritual* wholeness with God.

In none of these instances was the gift of Shalom understood to be an abstract ideal, or merely a feeling or a promise of some future heavenly bliss. Rather, salvation for Jesus always had a concrete and visible form. In his presence, people began to live in the fullness of their true, created purpose. Restored to wholeness, people were empowered to live transformed lives. In Christ we have the possibility of living in Shalom—good news, indeed!

Radiate God's love!

But what does all this mean in the humdrum of daily life? What does Shalom look like in the ordinary routines of our day? Nowhere do we get a clearer statement of the essence of Jesus' teachings, or a more concise summary of

> *"Who is a God like you, pardoning iniquity and passing over the transgression of the remnant of your possession? He does not retain his anger forever, because he delights in showing clemency. He will again have compassion upon us; he will tread our iniquities underfoot. You will cast all our sins into the depths of the sea."*
>
> Micah 7: 18-19

the meaning of Shalom for Christians, than in the Sermon on the Mount (Matthew 5-7). Here, in a few eloquent chapters, Jesus described the basic contours of Christian practice for those who have repented and have chosen to become his disciples.

As in all of his teaching, Jesus grounded his sermon in themes that his listeners immediately understood from their tradition. Then, as was his habit, Jesus turned those familiar themes inside out and upside down in surprising, fresh ways, so that nothing he said was exactly new, and yet everything he taught was revolutionary to the core.

The sermon begins with a series of blessings. After all, to live in Shalom is to enjoy fully God's deepest desires for humanity. Yet the blessings Jesus named as being characteristic of membership in his kingdom turn out to be a perplexing list indeed. Far from the promises of health-and-wealth promoted by so many modern evangelists, Jesus claimed that the people who are truly blessed are those in mourning, those who are weak and vulnerable, those who are passionate about living righteously. If you want to be blessed in the spirit of Shalom, he insisted, consider the merciful, the pure in heart, the peacemakers, or those who are enduring persecution because they are committed to doing good. These are the people who will experience the true Shalom of Christ's kingdom.

Jesus then continued in this paradoxical mode by inviting his listeners to reflect on ethical behavior and on the true nature of the Law. Those in the crowd, of course, knew the basic teachings of the Old Testament Law: good people do not commit adultery; good people do not steal; those who have been wronged can legitimately demand justice; you should be good to your friends and defend yourself against your enemies. On all of these points, right-thinking people would certainly be in agreement.

Yet Jesus once again challenged his audience to consider a completely new perspective on these old themes, a new worldview rooted in repentance and in an invitation to Shalom. According to the logic of the Sermon on the Mount, God's love—not self-preservation or the ego or coercion—is the most powerful force in the universe, and followers of Jesus should be ready to base every aspect of their lives on that standard.

With God's love as the baseline, Christian ethics take a radical turn away from the logic of reason and common sense. Thus, instead of merely avoiding adultery—a reasonable enough expectation—Jesus asked his followers not even to harbor lustful thoughts about the opposite sex, but to treat everyone with dignity and respect as a child of God. Instead of merely refraining from theft, Jesus taught his followers not even to covet another person's possessions since, too often, claims to private property become an obstacle to true Shalom. Instead of demanding the Old Testament justice of "an eye for an eye, and a tooth for a tooth," Jesus instructed his followers not to fight against their oppressors but to respond with generosity and kindness by giving the enemy even more than was demanded.

After all, as Jesus reminded his listeners, even immoral, unrighteous tax collectors are kind to their friends and spiteful to their enemies. Such behavior is commonplace; there's no hint of Shalom in that kind of behavior. Rather, Jesus invited his followers to take the unexpected step of loving their enemies and praying for those who persecuted them. Why? "So that you may be children of your Father in heaven" (Matthew 5:45). To live in this way is to claim your rightful inheritance as a child of God. This is the blueprint for Shalom restored.

On a mild winter's day in 1569, Dirk Willems escaped his second-story prison cell in a residential palace on the outskirts of the Dutch village of Asperen. Willems had been imprisoned for espousing heretical beliefs—among them adult, rather than infant, baptism and the principle of nonviolence. Many of Dirks' fellow believers, perhaps as many as 2,000 by the middle of the 16th century, had already been executed by Dutch magistrates. Hundreds more had been imprisoned and tortured for stubbornly persisting in their beliefs. Thus, when Dirk set foot on the icy moat surrounding his castle prison, he was literally running for his life.

What he had not expected, however, was that his escape would be noticed by the palace guard. Nor had he anticipated that the ice on which he now stood would be so thin. Almost as soon as the chase began, it was over. Dirk made it safely across the thin ice, but the heavier guard—burdened, no doubt, by his sword and armor—broke through. Fearing that he would drown, the guard called out for help. Defying all of his natural impulses to flee, Dirk returned and helped his pursuer out of the icy waters. In short order, Dirk was re-arrested and imprisoned at the top of a nearby church tower. On May 16, 1569, he was led to the edge of Asperen, bound to an upright pole, and burned to death as a heretic.

Dirk's action lays bare the simple premise behind Christ's radical teaching in the Sermon on the Mount: extend to others the same quality of love that God has extended to you.

This point becomes unmistakably clear in Jesus' reflections on the nature of prayer that follow in Matthew 6. In the Lord's Prayer, Jesus taught his disciples to pray daily that God's will and God's heavenly kingdom might be aligned with what is happening here on earth ("your kingdom come, your will be done on earth as it is in heaven"). Moreover, Jesus insisted that his followers were not to take God's forgiveness of their sins for granted. Indeed, when Christians pray the Lord's Prayer we put ourselves in an extremely vulnerable position by asking God to forgive us *in precisely the same way that we offer forgiveness to other people* ("forgive us our debts, as we also have forgiven our debtors"). It is not that we somehow earn God's forgiveness or our salvation by conscientiously forgiving other people. Jesus is not invoking here some new law that leads to a form of "works righteousness." But he is giving a very pointed warning against the opposite, more typical, temptation among Christians to think that salvation can come without repentance—that we can somehow casually claim God's forgiveness without nurturing a transformed attitude toward those who stand in need of our forgiveness.

Jesus could not possibly be clearer in his insistence that this is a false understanding of the gospel: "For if you forgive others their trespasses, your heavenly Father will also forgive you. *But if you do not forgive others, neither will your Father forgive your trespasses"* (Matthew 6:15).

All Things Old Are New Again!

Such is the nature of Jesus' new call to faithfulness. To be sure, his teachings drew heavily on images and themes from the Old Testament. The God who called Abram to leave behind the comforts of Ur is the same God who called Peter, James, and John to drop their nets and follow Jesus. He is the same God who calls us today to let go of our false forms of security and to trust completely in Christ.

God has not changed. His desire to restore humanity to its created purpose has remained constant throughout all of history. The Old Testament story offers a series of powerful hints regarding God's desire to reconcile humans to each other and to Himself. But the *fullness* of God's revelation to humanity is to be found in Christ and the message of the New Testament gospel. This may seem like an obvious point for most Christians, but it is especially relevant for those who see in the violence of the Old Testament a justification for Christians to participate in warfare today.

In Christ, the Old Testament themes of God inviting His people toward the fullness of Shalom have not been forgotten, but they have been *transformed*. Thus, Jesus clearly affirmed the Covenant between God and His people as a basis for the relationship of trust and obedience that believers have today with their Creator. Yet at the same time, he explicitly expanded the boundaries of the Covenant far beyond ethnic Judaism to include *everyone* who was willing to repent and was ready to follow Jesus— Samaritans, women, tax collectors, fishermen, prostitutes, Zealots, and lepers. In Christ, the promise of the new Covenant, the promise of Shalom, extends beyond racial and cultural boundaries. "For God so loved the world that He gave His only Son, so that everyone who believes in Him may not perish but may have eternal life" (John 3:16).

Similarly, Jesus was respectful of the Old Testament Law, insisting that he did not come to ridicule or abolish the structure and coherence it provided to Jewish society. Yet at the same time, he reminded his listeners that the Law must always be in service to the higher good of Shalom. The entire Old Testament Law, he taught, could be reduced to two basic principles, both of which point toward Shalom: "Love the Lord your God with all your heart, soul, mind and strength"; and "Love your neighbor as yourself" (Mark 12:30-31).

Jesus clearly fit within the Old Testament tradition of the godly king, exemplified by David, who balanced royal power with righteousness and justice. Yet the deeper nature of Christ's kingship turned standard notions of political power completely upside down. In resisting the temptations of Satan at the beginning of his ministry, for example, Jesus made it clear that he would not use his power in manipulative ways. He would not become a welfare king by turning stones into bread or create a spectacle by jumping off the temple tower. Nor would he be seduced by the allure of political grandeur Satan offered him as king over a vast empire.

Later in his ministry, when Peter—who had just recognized Jesus as the Christ—rejected the idea that the Messiah might suffer or actually be put to death, Jesus sharply rebuked him. He went on to remind the disciples once again that anyone interested in being one of his followers must be prepared to "deny themselves and take up their cross . . . . For those who want to save their life will lose it, and those who lose their life for my sake, and for the sake of the gospel, will save it" (Mark 8:34-35). To the very end, Jesus refused popular pressure to assume the mantle of a revolutionary warrior, making his triumphal entry into Jerusalem on the back of a donkey rather than on a white stallion, and instructing Peter in the Garden of Gethsemane to put away his sword.

It would be incorrect to claim that Jesus was somehow apolitical, since his teaching agitated Jewish authorities so deeply and the Romans executed him as a criminal. But the source of his political power came not from the strength of his armies or from the coercive nature of his strategies. Instead, he called his followers to nurture the vulnerable practices of Shalom and to live consistently according to the principles of love and compassion. And this new form of politics—the politics of Jesus—eventually transformed the world.

A Violent Death . . . and a Triumphant Resurrection

Like many of us today, Jesus' disciples found his message powerfully attractive. Yet they struggled to understand what it would mean to take his teachings seriously, to actually apply them in daily life. In reading through the gospel narratives, one can sense a growing urgency and frustration in Jesus as his journey brought him closer to Jerusalem and his impending crucifixion. The disciples often seemed to be so close to grasping the upside-down message of Shalom, yet repeatedly they would say or do things that made it clear they had still not fully understood the radical message Jesus was trying to teach them.

Love, not deadly force, is the Christian's weapon.

Just before his fateful entrance into Jerusalem, for example, Jesus called his disciples aside and reminded them once again of the suffering and humiliation that awaited him. Yet almost immediately James and John fell into an argument about who would have the seat of honor when Jesus "came into his glory." No! Jesus replied. Obviously, they still had not understood. They were still thinking in the fashion of ordinary rulers and officials. So once more Jesus reminded them that in his new kingdom of Shalom "whoever wishes to become great among you must be your servant, and whoever wishes to be first must be slave of all" (Mark 10:43-44).

In his final meal together with the disciples, Jesus tried once again to model the character of true power in his kingdom by kneeling before each of his disciples and washing their feet. But even here, the paradox of power perfected in weakness and love seems to have eluded their understanding.

There is a standard Protestant account of the crucifixion, and the events leading up to it, that can sometimes sound almost saccharine-sweet in the telling—an image of Jesus as a sacrificial lamb, passively and dutifully playing out his divinely appointed role so that we might enjoy salvation. Yet there is nothing gentle or pastoral in the story of Christ's crucifixion. It is impossible to read the account of Jesus in the Garden of Gethsemane without feeling the depth of his anguish or the agony in his temptation to renounce his mission altogether ("let this cup pass from me").

No one should think that the path of Shalom is easy, or that Christ's way of peace comes without emotional and physical costs. The blatant injustice of his sham trial, Peter's denial of his friendship, the humiliation of his journey to Golgotha, the intense physical suffering of his crucifixion—all this flies in the face of our sense of fairness and justice. In the final moments before his death, Jesus himself wondered whether God had abandoned him. And he wrestled with the thought of calling down the forces of heaven to resist the apparent victory of raw, coercive violence over his vision of Shalom.

And yet, to the very end, Jesus was unyielding in his commitment to the principles of love and peace. "Father, forgive them," he prayed on behalf of his executioners, "for they do not know what they are doing" (Luke 23:34).

For nearly two millennia, Christians have debated the precise theological meaning of Christ's death on the cross. Many have come to regard the crucifixion as the result of a complex deal that God made with Himself. Since humans are sinful and incapable of meriting God's love, they clearly deserve to be punished. But because Jesus, a completely sinless human being, offered himself as a sacrifice on our behalf, the debt we owe to God for our sins has been paid in full. Thus, Jesus came to earth primarily to die on the cross. In so doing, he balanced, on our behalf, God's need for justice. Such a reading of the crucifixion is not without theological merit. But it is clearly only a *part* of the story.

Another, often overlooked, dimension of Christ's crucifixion situates it within the much broader context of the biblical story of Shalom. Since the Fall, humans have lived under the powerful illusion that in order to establish their security, they will find themselves at war with God, with each other, and with nature itself. All of life, we tell ourselves, is a struggle for survival, with victory ultimately going to the strongest, the fittest, the most powerful, the most cunning. But alongside this version of human history, written in the blood of warfare and violence, is another story—the story of God's persistent efforts to call humans back to their true purpose, the story of God inviting us to live as we were intended to live, to live in Shalom.

This perspective suggests a reading of the crucifixion which is nuanced somewhat differently from the standard Protestant account. It is not a blood-thirsty God demanding a sacrifice that brought Christ to the cross, but rather a violent and evil world that could not abide his message of compassion. Yes, Christ suffered on our behalf, but his agony and suffering is more a testimony to the genuine reality of evil in a world driven by the logic of violence and power than it is to God's demand for a blood sacrifice. The way of the cross is an inevitable consequence for all those who are ready to follow Jesus on the vulnerable path of love and compassion.

Even more to the point, the crucifixion, as all Christians know, is only part of the Easter story. The dramatic climax of the gospel narrative is actually not Christ's death on Good Friday—after all, countless other good people have died cruel deaths. Rather, the main point of the Passion Story, the axis around which the whole gospel turns, is Christ's *resurrection* on Easter Sunday. When, Jesus rose from the dead on the third day—just as he told his disciples he would—God announced to the world that the powers of evil and violence do not have the final word. The resurrection was the vindication of God's ultimate triumph of love over the forces of violence. It guarantees to all those who follow in the humble way of Christ, that in the end—against all odds and contrary to the logic of human reason—Shalom will indeed prevail. Christ's resurrection from the dead is God's affirmation of a revolutionary kind of power, a power made perfect in weakness. "Don't be afraid," goes the refrain of the song, "my love is stronger than your fears."

And so it is. Christians are people who live on *this* side of the resurrection, knowing that God's love has already triumphed over death. To say "yes" to Jesus is to live each day in the confidence that the victory over coercion and violence has already been won.

This is the good news of the gospel. For a world that so often seems hopelessly locked into cycles of violence and domination, for nations willing to sacrifice their youth to defend borders and ideals, for individuals who are trapped in roles as oppressors and victims—to all who are paralyzed by fear—the resurrection holds the promise that Christ's way of Shalom is the way to true life.

In many Christian circles today, pacifism is regarded as an ideology promoted for partisan political reasons or as an eccentric detour in Christian theology. Many Christians have regarded this message of peace as an optional add-on to the core of the gospel, championed by a handful of sectarian groups who have not had to face the heavy responsibilities of maintaining political order. The central burden of this chapter—an abbreviated overview of the biblical story from Creation to the resurrection—is to suggest that the way of peace is at the very heart of the gospel and of Christian faith. Such an understanding of faith begins with a hardheaded, unflinching awareness of the pervasive character of evil in the world. But it refuses to allow the coercive nature of evil to have the final word. Instead, through God's acts of compassion throughout history, through the life and teachings of Christ, and through the power of the resurrection, Christians are able to live in the Shalom that God deeply desires for all of humanity.

This is the Christian difference. This is the good news of Jesus Christ.

Yes, But . . .

By now some readers may be prepared to say: "Yes, it does make sense that those who have received God's gracious gift of love and have chosen to follow Christ should not kill other people," or "Yes, God's forgiveness should lead us to forgive others, including our enemies." But almost as quickly comes the thought that even though it may sound compelling, it still seems so unrealistic. What would the world look like if everyone in authority thought like this? What about my Christian friends or relatives—people I respect and trust—who are currently serving in the armed forces or who, perhaps, have died in combat? What would it mean to those relationships if pacifism suddenly became central to my understanding of Christian faith?

Or perhaps all this simply sounds too difficult, too heroic. This was not what you bargained for when you decided to become a Christian. This wasn't part of the package.

"But more than that, we even boast in God through our Lord Jesus Christ, through whom we have now received reconciliation."
Romans 5:11

If you are inclined toward some variation of these thoughts, I invite you to consider the following concluding reflections. These are not airtight arguments designed to back you into a corner. Think of them instead as seeds that may find room to germinate in your mind as you reflect on Christ's teachings and as you continue to explore God's leading in your Christian walk.

(1) Jesus anticipated that his radical message might strain the bonds of family and friendship. When he told his

disciples, "I have not come to bring peace, but a sword" (Matthew 10:34), Jesus was not suddenly reversing his teachings on love for the enemy. Rather, he was reminding his disciples that the radical nature of repentance might well force painful decisions about the natural ties of allegiance that they had with their biological families.

The words that follow that eye-catching claim—"I have come to set a man against his father, a daughter against her mother, a daughter-in-law against her mother-in-law . . . . Whoever loves father or mother more than me is not worthy of me"—only underscore the stark contrast that Jesus was drawing between the life-changing call of discipleship and the natural bonds of affection that tie us to our families, tradition, and culture.

The point is not that we should live in permanent hostility with our families, or that natural bonds of affection are inherently evil. But the nature of our allegiances must be unmistakably clear. And in some circumstances, Christ's call will take precedence over our relationships with family and friends.

(2) To all Christians who are not yet convinced that love of enemies is part of God's good news of salvation, I would urge you to ask the question: "What, exactly, is the Christian witness in the face of violence?" Do we have anything unique to offer that wouldn't be shared by a decent, moral non-Christian?

Surely you do not have to be a Christian to recognize that violence should be restrained (as Jesus said, "even the righteous heathen" teach this). Surely you do not have to be a Christian to show kindness to your neighbor while supporting strong military solutions against our enemies.

As we have seen, the principles of Just War were all developed in their basic outline by the Roman philosopher

Cicero, a thoughtful pagan who derived these ideas on the basis of reason. So the question remains: In the crucial matter of violence against our enemies, what is the *Christian* witness to the world? What is the *Christian* difference?

(3) There are many Christians, perhaps longstanding and faithful followers of Christ, who have never regarded pacifism as an essential part of Christ's teachings. The point of the invitation I am making in this chapter is not to belittle the integrity of these believers' commitments to Christ or to suggest that their Christian ministry has been without fruits. Still, each one of us is on a journey of new understandings and insights. I believe that God's desire for Shalom may be calling such people to an even deeper level of fellowship with Christ.

The Shalom of embodied love, especially loving one's enemy, is a central—I think, essential—feature of the gospel. For these Christians, this good news might simply expand their awareness of God's miraculous presence, and it may satisfy a yearning for a commitment and trust that goes deeper than the blessings they already enjoy. In such a case, my goal is not to compel agreement but to invite reconsideration.

For more reflections on appropriate "etiquette" among Christians who hold profound differences, and an honest acknowledgment of the practical limits of pacifism, I encourage you to continue reading.

---

[1] Drawn extensively from the account of the story by Stanley Green, "When Reconciled, We are Free," *Mennonite Weekly Review*, Sept. 7, 2000, 4.

4.

A CASE FOR
PACIFIST HUMILITY

"Now we see in a mirror, dimly, but then we will see face to face."

I Corinthians 13:12

One recent summer evening, I was walking through the campus of Goshen College with my nine-year-old daughter. It was a warm and pleasant night; the stars were in brilliant array and I had just commented on the beauty of the moonlight shining through the leafy trees, when I suddenly came to an abrupt stop. There, silhouetted above some benches on the edge of an open plaza, I could see the shadowy figure of a man hiding behind a tree and the clear outline of a gun in his hand. Instantly, I grabbed hold of my daughter's hand and pulled her close to me. My anxiety edged toward terror when I began to make out other shadowy persons in the dark, pressed down close to the ground.

And then, in a sudden flash, I realized what was going on. These were not criminal predators stalking the campus, but only a group of high school kids, each carrying a toy laser gun and wearing some sort of device that would

---

sound an alarm whenever they came into the path of some-one else's laser.

When I realized that the mysterious figures were not actual killers—only teenagers pretending to kill—the adrenaline rush of my original fear turned almost instantly to anger. Without hesitating, I called the young people to come out of the shadows and I demanded to know what they were doing. They were merely "playing a game—like tag," one of them said. "Tag?!" I yelled in response. And with scarcely a pause I launched into a veritable harangue: "This was not tag! This was not play! Guns are designed to kill people! Young people your age are dying all the time in the streets! Your game makes a mockery of their deaths! This campus is an extension of my home! I want to be able to walk around at night and feel safe here! Don't you real-ize that we are pacifists here? We believe in peace! It's wrong to desecrate the campus of Goshen College with war games like this. What could you possibly have been thinking?!"

The group that had gathered by now looked on ner-vously, uncertain how to respond as I finally paused to take a breath. But my speech was not yet over. When someone among them ventured that he "respected my ideology, but I should respect their freedom," I sputtered that my reli-gious convictions were not some "ideology," and then I proceeded to denounce his notion of "freedom" as little more than self-indulgent individualism gone to seed.

Seeing that I was convincing no one, I eventually gave a final snort of indignation and continued on my sorrowful way. But even before I got to our house, the irony of my encounter was already coming home to roost in my con-science. The teenagers were simply looking for some late-night recreation—a harmless group activity, in their minds—and I had turned the campus into an arena of moral superiority. They had left the encounter not persuaded by my rhetoric but, more than likely, angry and shamed by my public scolding. How stupid of me to think that someone could be convinced of the merits of pacifism through a verbal version of fisticuffs. I dropped my daughter off at home and turned around to go back and apologize. But they were already long gone.

My brief encounter that warm summer night points to a much deeper challenge facing all Christians, but especially to those seeking to be faithful to Christ's way of peace. On the one hand, we live in a culture of moral relativism where truth is often regarded as little more than arbitrary cultural norms or the accident of personal opinion. For many modern people the only absolute in life is the right of every individual to define truth for her- or himself. In such a context, people of faith dare not be silenced, fearful that their convictions regarding God's living presence in the world and His purposes for humanity will be ridiculed or inevitably cause offense.

As Jesus discovered in his "cleansing" of the temple and in his confrontations with the Sadducees and Pharisees, naming the truth boldly in public settings can easily upset a lot of people. In a similar manner, because the language of Christian nonviolence disrupts the logic of a Nietzschean worldview, advocates for peace will almost certainly be a thorn in the flesh for those with a vested interest in maintaining the status quo. In a culture virtually incapable of making moral distinctions, the Christian witness needs to be heard now more than ever.

At the same time, however, the painful legacy of the Christian Crusades and the many ways in which God's name has been abused by the powerful should prompt all of us toward the side of caution. Claiming to know God's will for humanity can all too easily lead Christians to adopt a style of witness that goes well beyond confident testimony to arrogance and imperialism. As history has demonstrated all too frequently, people who claim to speak in the name of God have often not been afraid to back up their convictions with violence.

For this reason, Christians need to make their case to an indifferent or hostile world in a manner and style that is consistent with the nature of the Christ they claim to serve. Too often, as I was forced to recognize in myself, Christians—and perhaps especially Christian pacifists—can slip into a tone of arrogance and belligerence. We can be so self-assured of the moral superiority of our cause that we lose sight of the fact that Christ's way of peace calls us to respect the dignity of all people, including those who seem to be our enemies.

Thus, arguments for Christian pacifism that seek to win their case through rhetorical bluster or crafty forms of logical manipulation have missed the whole point. In its very essence, Christian faith is invitational rather than coercive. If, indeed, God intended humans to live in peace with each

> "If only there were evil people somewhere insidiously committing evil deeds, and it were necessary only to separate them from the rest of us and destroy them! But the line dividing good and evil cuts through the heart of every human being. And who is willing to destroy a piece of his own heart?"
>
> Alexander Solzhenitsyn

other, if the ideal of Shalom is embedded into the very grain of the universe, then Christian faith dare not be represented as a series of logical propositions that need to be argued with tactical cleverness and white-knuckled intensity. Instead, since we are confident that our faith is anchored in the truth, all we need to do is bear witness to that truth in an invitational and noncoercive manner.

The challenge facing all of us, but most especially pacifist Christians, is to negotiate our way in modern culture between the temptation to assert the truth with absolute certainty and the equally tempting impulse to retreat into an open-ended relativism incapable of making moral commitments or meaningful ethical choices.

The questions I want to explore in this chapter might be summarized as follows: Is it possible for a Christian to maintain deep convictions about divine truth and God's will for the world, while simultaneously acknowledging that our particular understandings are limited and partial? Can we hold passionate beliefs about God that do not ultimately promote some form of violence? Alternatively, can we openly admit that "we see through a glass darkly" without slipping down the slope of relativism?

I believe that such a posture is not only possible, but essential, if Christianity is to survive as a vibrant, living reality in the world, rather than merely one more isolated subculture in a fragmented postmodern society.

The key to this challenge, I suggest, can be found in the Christian proclamation of a noncoercive Christ who provides a bridge across the postmodern gulf between violence and relativism. We often are accustomed to thinking of pacifism primarily in a context of war or physical violence. In this chapter I want to broaden our understanding of Christ's way of peace beyond a series of strategies or behaviors. At its essence, Christian pacifism is a mode of being in the world that shapes our inner spirit as well as our deeds, our attitudes as well as our actions.

Furthermore, the gospel of peace should have profound consequences not only for how we respond to situations of conflict, but for our understanding of missions as well. For if we are witnessing to a God whose power is expressed most profoundly through the vulnerability of the cross, then the recipients of our testimony need not fear that the gospel we are bringing will be oppressive or violent. Liberated from service to national identity, to promises of wealth, to status or to power, Christ's way of peace can offer non-Christians a freedom from sin that is genuinely liberating.

Humility: A Christian Alternative?

In describing this position, it may be helpful to shift our attention from the language of pacifism to a closely related virtue, one that better captures the qualities of pacifism as a way of being, rather than an ethical strategy or behavior—that is, the Christian posture of *humility*.

To introduce the language of humility into American Christianity is a risky proposition. Many contemporary Christians, especially evangelicals, are much more comfortable with a rhetorical style characterized by sharp-angled beliefs, clearly stated doctrines, and a robust and virile faith—a faith that is assertive and goal-directed. In the American setting, humility sounds like a religion for wimps. It conjures up images of melba milquetoasts or emotional weaklings who go through life wearing permanent Kick Me signs.

As I want to suggest in more detail later in the book, such is emphatically not the case. Christian pacifists are people who are indeed clear about convictions, capable of drawing lines, and able to make tough choices that testify to God's power in the world. True Christian humility should never be confused with the false humility of a moral relativist who ends up saying, "I don't know the truth, but you don't know it either, so let's just agree to be nice to each other."

At the same time, however, a faith infused with humility is deeply aware of its own vulnerability both before God and the world. The humility of a Christian pacifist consciously cultivates an active trust in God that "leans not on our own understanding." It greets each day with the anticipation of new revelations of God's Shalom, and it openly welcomes the surprise that comes from God's intervention into our own best-laid plans.

Talking about humility, of course, always involves a bit of a paradox. The moment you define it, or highlight a certain action as embodying its qualities, you realize that you have somehow violated its very essence. So it may be more helpful to start by identifying what humility is not.

Christian humility is not an affirmation of abuse or low self-esteem. It is not a retreat from the world's suffering and pain or a shrinking back from all expressions of power.

To the contrary, Christian humility begins with a positive assertion: We are children of God, made in God's image, created for Shalom. As God's own creation we have an inherent dignity and status that cannot be taken away by any human being or earthly power. Indeed, precisely because we are confident about our divine status—a status conferred on us by God, not by ourselves, our achievements, other people, or the state—we can adopt a posture of vulnerability and love in all circumstances, even when confronted by people who threaten us. Christian humility is a voluntary letting go of coercive power in a way that reflects the very character of God. Its best exemplar can be found in the person of Jesus Christ.

"The Servant Is Not Greater than His Master"

From the miraculous events surrounding his birth to the dramatic story of his death and resurrection, Jesus embodied humility throughout his entire life. He entered the world under the humblest of circumstances. Born into a poor, obscure Jewish family, he and his parents lived initially as refugees in Egypt before returning to a homeland dominated by a Roman occupying army. Throughout his active ministry Jesus consistently associated with people at the fringes of respectable society—foreigners, tax-collectors, laborers, prostitutes, and children—refusing to put on airs or to consider himself too pious or holy to risk being seen with marginalized people.

Those actions were consistent with his preaching, in which admonitions to humility and service echoed throughout his entire public ministry. In the Sermon on the Mount, for example, Jesus startled his listeners by teaching that the people who are truly blessed are likely to be the meek, the lowly of heart, and the persecuted (Matthew 5:3-10). In his kingdom, normal assumptions regarding status and privilege were reversed. Here, the "first will be last, and the last will be first" (Mark 10:31).

Jesus had to repeat these teachings so frequently, in part at least, because his disciples were very slow to understand the upside-down nature of his messianic message. Once, when Jesus found his disciples arguing among themselves over who was the greatest, he put an end to their squabbling by embracing a child: "Whoever welcomes one such child in my name welcomes me," he told them (Mark 9: 33-37). Yet only a short while later, James and John came to Jesus hoping to be given special status in the new kingdom they expected him to establish in Jerusalem. Again Jesus reminded them that true power was characterized by humility: "Whoever wishes to become great among you must be your servant, and whoever wishes to be first among you must be slave of all" (Mark 10:43-44; Luke 22:25-27; Matthew 20:25-28). Later, confronting the Pharisees, Jesus repeated his warnings against the kind of power that rested on titles or ceremonies or positions of honor: "All who exalt themselves will be humbled, and all who humble themselves will be exalted" (Matthew 23:12).

No event in Jesus' life better illustrates this consistent motif of humility than the story of his crucifixion. Before the cheers of an exultant Jewish crowd looking for a powerful king, Jesus entered Jerusalem on a lowly donkey. At the celebration of the Passover, Jesus gathered his disciples for a final meal together. Here, in his last opportunity to offer a concluding bit of teaching, Jesus assumed the role of a servant and began to wash the dirty feet of his weary followers. When Peter protested against this posture of humility, Jesus reminded the group once more that this was precisely how they were to treat each other: "I have set you an example that you also should do as I have done to you. Very truly, I tell you, servants are not greater than their master, nor are messengers greater than the one who sent them. If you know these things, you are blessed if you do them" (John 13:15-17).

Later, in the painful moments of anxiety and self-doubt in the Garden of Gethsemane, Jesus submitted himself yet again to the unfolding will of God and gave his body over to the forces of coercion and violence.

Humility as modeled by Jesus, therefore, has both an inward and an outward expression. As an internal spiritual reality, humility calls us repeatedly to prayer in the daily yielding of ourselves to God's will. In the Lord's Prayer, Christians ask that God's will be done "on earth as it is in heaven," which is to say that we seek to conform our purposes and priorities here on earth with those of God's. We see this same spirit in the agonizing words of Jesus in the Garden of Gethsamane where he prayed fervently that God might provide an alternative to his suffering and death. Yet in the end, Jesus yielded himself fully to God, praying "not what I want, but what you want" (Matthew 26:39).

The outward, more tangible, expressions of Christian humility can be seen in the daily cultivation of the practices of love, compassion, hospitality, and service to others in the church and to our neighbors in the world.

Humility hardly seems like a suitable foundation for teaching with any authority or for inaugurating a new social movement. Yet in their witness to Christ's redemptive purpose in the world, the apostles and the early church consistently described Jesus as someone whose spiritual authority remained unquestioned—indeed was even confirmed—by his human weakness and vulnerability.

One of the church's earliest confessions of faith, a beautiful hymn recorded in Philippians 2, identifies Christ's humility as the very essence of his character. Those who follow in Christ's footsteps, wrote Paul, should "do nothing out of selfish ambition or vain conceit, but in humility consider others better than yourselves" (NIV). What better model for this could we have, he continued, than Jesus Christ himself:

> *"Who, though he was in the form of God, did not regard equality with God as something to be exploited, but emptied himself, taking the form of a slave, being born in human likeness. And being found in human form, he humbled himself and became obedient to the point of death—even death on a cross."*
>
> **Philippians 2:6-8**

Paul, himself hardly a shrinking violet, could face his own limitations by acknowledging that God's power is often "made perfect in weakness" (2 Corinthians 12:9). In Colossians, Paul admonished those "who have been raised with Christ" to clothe themselves "with compassion, kindness, humility, meekness, and patience" (Colossians 3:12). The characteristics of the mature Christian he listed in Galatians—"love, joy, peace, patience, kindness, generosity, faithfulness, gentleness, and self-control"—only further underscore the centrality of these virtues (Galatians 5:22).

At the same time, however, Paul clearly recognized that suffering is not itself the goal of Christian humility. Believers are not being called to diminish into insignificance or to seek out physical pain as an end in itself. Rather, hidden within the posture of voluntary humility is a paradoxical form of power and strength and honor. For in our humility we recognize our absolute dependence on God and we are called back to our deepest selves—the vulnerability and trust of Shalom which God intended for us at creation.

It is crucial, then, that the hymn recorded in Philippians 2 does not end with Jesus dying on the cross. Instead, it concludes on a note of victory and joy because Jesus willingly humbled himself:

". . . God also highly exalted him and gave him the name that is above every name, so that at the name of Jesus every knee should bend, in heaven and on earth and under the earth, and every tongue should confess that Jesus Christ is Lord, to the glory of God the Father."

Philippians 2:9-11

A posture of Christian humility invites us to love other people in the same way that God has loved us in Christ: noncoercively, gently, creatively, vulnerably, invitationally. Humility is the concrete embodiment of our confidence that God loves us and that God is in control of human history.

Throughout the ages Christians have at least paid lip service to the virtue of humility, even if they have not always been clear about its actual relevance in the world. For Christian pacifists, however, humility is not simply a lofty abstraction nor an ideal to be seriously cultivated only by the professional clergy or those in monastic orders. For those committed to Christ's way of peace, humility is a way of being in the world that permeates an entire worldview and decisively shapes our thoughts and actions. To live in Shalom is to cultivate humility in every aspect of life.

We live in a culture where differences are frequently resolved either by violence or by a disengaged retreat into relativism. I have suggested that the posture of humility offers Christians a third option for responding to conflict, an alternative that neither imposes its way on the world nor evades all moral responsibility. Let me turn then to some specific forms that humility assumes for Christians intent on pursuing this third way.

Eschatological Humility

Eschatology refers simply to the Christian awareness that history is unfolding according to God's plan, and that God is ultimately in control of the outcome. From an eschatological perspective, Christians are called to discern God's will in their daily lives, to be responsible caretakers of God's creation, and to align themselves with God's movement in history. But ultimately it is God who is in the driver's seat.

In principle, most Christians would readily agree with the claim that God, not humans, is in control of history's outcome. After all, this is why we pray—to acknowledge God's power and presence in shaping our lives. But, as most of us know, actually living day-to-day in an attitude of permanent trust, leaving the outcome of history in God's hands, is a more difficult challenge than merely affirming it as a general principle. We tend to resent our lack of certainty about the future because it reminds us of the limits of our own power and fuels a sense of insecurity and vulnerability. Our natural inclination is to seek ways of gaining a greater sense of control over our lives, especially over the future.

One way of controlling the future is to pore over passages in scripture that seem to offer hints about the date and details of Christ's return. Some Christians have focused an enormous amount of energy on studying the books of Daniel or Revelation in an effort to reveal the precise details of God's plans for the future. Such efforts, however, are often only a symptom of our insecurity, our unwillingness to leave the future in God's hands. Jesus made it clear that "no one knows the day or the hour of the Lord's return," yet our resistance to the unknown feeds a desire to break the code and to nail down exactly where we stand in relation to the final days.

Even more commonly, humans seek to close off the open-ended horizons of the future by relying on the modern insights of the social sciences—sociologists, economists, political scientists, and psychologists whose empirical rigor and scientific analysis may enable us to predict the future and to control our own eschatology.

The desire to shape the outcome of history is a basic human impulse. We fear the unknown and our lack of control. Yet this very desire to control the future is at the heart of the problem of human violence. People who turn to violence nearly always do so with the assumption that they know how history *should* turn out. Violence is a tool humans use to ensure that their vision of the future will prevail over someone else's or, as is more often the case, will prevail over some unknown outcome.

When Christians justify the use of violence they are no longer seeking to find their place in God's invitation to Shalom. Instead, they are seizing control of history's outcome and insisting that their vision of the future must be enacted, even if it means killing other people along the way to do so.

Eschatological humility, by contrast, accepts the fact that all of life is sustained by God; that "God's ways are not our ways"; that we live every day in trust and dependence on God, seeking to align ourselves with God's movement in history without claiming to know in advance the conclusion of any given event. Such a posture is central to Christian faith in general, but it is absolutely essential for the Christian pacifist.

Eschatological humility makes no claims about the effectiveness of pacifism in yielding a specific result. It may be that the enemy will miraculously be disarmed by love or a creative alternative to violence. But it is also possible that a pacifist response will entail physical suffering, as has been the case for thousands of Christian martyrs. Either way, however, eschatological humility calls us to participate with Jesus, both in the agonizing uncertainty of the Garden of Gethsemane and in the joyous triumph of the resurrection.

Epistemological Humility

Epistemology, like eschatology, is a $50 word not ordinarily used in friendly conversation. But it helpfully identifies a second important expression of humility that thoughtful Christians should seek to embrace. Epistemology refers to the foundations of our perceptions about reality: On what basis do we actually know what we claim to know? What is the final grounding or foundation for the arguments we make about our doctrine, faith, or life?

Philosophers over the centuries have offered a host of insightful and complex arguments regarding epistemology. The standard answer to such questions, especially for modern people living in democracies, is that our understanding of reality is ultimately based on the human capacity for reason. Since the time of Plato, many philosophers have argued that the ability to reason is somehow hardwired into humans, making it possible for people from different backgrounds and cultures to have meaningful conversations and to reach agreements on how they will live together.

Reason enables all healthy people to gather evidence, recognize meaningful patterns in that evidence, offer arguments based on logic, and eventually arrive at the same conclusions. Since the European Enlightenment of the seventeenth and eighteenth centuries, reason has been the foundation for most political discourse. And it has typically been the way Christians have argued about doctrine and engaged in missions as well: gather your evidence, marshal your Bible verses, make a tightly constructed rational argument, anticipate all the loopholes, and the powerful logic of the persuasive Christian point of view will, in effect, force your discussion partners to concede the point.

An epistemology based on reason has proven to be a very effective tool for much of modern life. And, as part of God's created order, reason can point humans—Christians and non-Christians alike—in the direction of Shalom. But at the same time, a pacifist Christian will be cautious about grounding Christian faith or Christ's way of peace on the foundation of reason's persuasive logic. If God's Truth must ultimately stand or fall at the bar of reason, then humans can very easily transform God into little more than a projection of our own best thoughts or well-crafted plans.

A faith based on reason can quickly reduce Christianity to a series of precisely worded doctrinal statements to be rationally understood and logically demonstrated, along the lines of a legal brief. An epistemology of reason leads us to think that the Christian case can be demonstrated by rational proof and that the inexorable power of our arguments can back the unsaved into a logical corner or an irrational dead end. As such, rational arguments for Christianity very easily become subtle forms of coercion.

Epistemological humility does not call the Christian to willful ignorance, nor does it discard rationality as inherently evil. But it does recognize the profound limits of reason as the primary means by which Christians testify to the presence of God. Those who are committed to a nonviolent understanding of the gospel will be much more likely to think of missions in terms of simply "bearing witness" to

"Do not repay anyone evil for evil . . . Do not take revenge, but leave room for God's wrath."
Romans 12:17, 19 (NIV)

the truth as they have experienced it in their own lives. Such an approach assumes that the truth of God's gift of grace and forgiveness is best served, not by getting our logical proofs straight, but by following Jesus; not by crafting powerful arguments and winning a debate, but simply by committing ourselves to exemplify Christ's love in the daily routines of our lives together.

The vulnerability of a Christian pacifist should find expression not only in our actions, but also in the manner and tone of our engagement with those who disagree. My arguments to the teenagers playing laser tag made perfectly good sense to me. I think they were all valid and reasonable considerations that should have been persuasive. But it would have been a much more consistent witness to Christian humility if I had adopted a tone that invited them into conversation and had simply shared my convictions in the form of a testimony.

If the gospel of Christ is indeed the truth, then we need not defend it in ways that compel agreement—either through the force of arms or through the demands of reason. Instead, epistemological humility calls us simply to live out the good news of the gospel in our daily lives, to be prepared to testify to the transforming power of Christ in our lives, to offer witness to the power of the cross and resurrection, and then to allow God to change people's hearts so that, as with the early church in Acts, "day by day the Lord added to their number those who were being saved" (Acts 2:47).

Ethical Humility

In the early sixteenth century, the Swiss reformer Ulrich Zwingli successfully introduced the Reformation in the city of Zurich where he had been serving as its leading Catholic priest. His victory was complicated, however, by the fact that some of his early supporters were now taking him to task for compromising the authority of "Scripture alone" *(sola Scriptura)*. The Anabaptists, as this group became known, insisted that true Christians should follow the path of Jesus even if it meant sharing freely of their possessions and renouncing the sword.

Zwingli responded that these sixteenth-century pacifists had gone too far. Instead of accepting God's salvation as a free gift, he argued, they were introducing a new form of monasticism into Protestant circles. Their insistence on such high moral standards threatened to overshadow God's grace and impose a burden of moral perfectionism that no average Christian could seriously be expected to follow.

I think Zwingli was wrong in his critique. Yet Christian pacifists should not be too quick to dismiss his concern about works-righteousness. Ethical humility reminds pacifists who sometimes slip into moral pride or the illusion of perfectionism that they too stand before God in daily need of His forgiveness and grace. After all, even those who sacrificed their lives as martyrs did not die in a state of ethical perfection.

In a similar way, ethical humility should keep pacifists from pretending that their way of life is totally free from every form of violence and coercion. The complex interrelatedness of modern life and the pervasive nature of structural violence—evident in unjust economic relations, deeply-rooted racism, unfair access to political power, and so on—virtually guarantee that all of us are implicated in some forms of coercion, even if we are not personally inflicting violence on others.

Ethical humility demands, for example, that I recognize my complicity in a punitive and sometimes unfair criminal justice system simply by virtue of being a tax-paying citizen. Even though I could not in good conscience own a gun or use lethal violence, ethical humility demands that I acknowledge that my personal security is frequently enhanced by the police officer's billy club and the mere existence of the armed forces.

Ethical humility further obliges me to recognize the compromises I have made with the ideal of absolute noncoercion in human relations. I have, for example, spanked my children; I would advocate the physical restraint of a deranged person; I pay taxes, some of which support the military.

I do think that there is a fundamental dividing line between coercive force and lethal violence. I want to minimize the former, while rejecting absolutely the latter. But I do not pretend that my commitment to Christian pacifism has made me ethically pure or that pacifists have achieved some measure of moral perfectionism.

Christian pacifists need to acknowledge that their lives fall far short of the ideals of the kingdom of heaven. Although this principle of ethical humility should never become a rationale for justifying "cheap grace"—a grace that forgives the sin instead of the sinner—it should remind us that all of our actions pale in comparison to the glory of God.

In the end, the goal of Christian pacifism is not to achieve high marks from God at the judgment day, but only to offer a testimony—flawed and imperfect though it may be—to the nature of God's love for humanity. So, with appropriate humility, we "press on to take hold of that for which Christ Jesus took hold of [us]." (Philippians 3:12b, *NIV*).

> *"True evangelical faith cannot lie dormant. It clothes the naked, feeds the hungry, comforts the sorrowful, shelters the destitute, serves those that harm it, binds up that which is wounded, it has become all things to all people."*
> — Menno Simons, 1539

Humility of Respectful Dissent

Finally, a Christian pacifist will cultivate humility when engaging in conversation with those who disagree. The position I am taking in this book—that pacifism is the essence of the Christian gospel—will undoubtedly strike many Christians as a brash and unsettling claim. This may be especially true of Christians whose families have had a long tradition of service in the armed forces and have always regarded those commitments as a source of family identity and pride. Likewise, arguments for pacifism coming in times of war or heightened political tensions may sound disloyal or even treasonous to some readers.

The humility of respectful dissent calls Christian pacifists to listen carefully to the concerns raised by their opponents. It calls for a sensitivity in language and tone that can appropriately shift from the bold and prophetic to the gentle and pastoral. It suggests a willingness to absorb the anger and resentment of people who look on pacifists in general as naïve freeloaders and cowards or as a blight on the national well-being. And it might even require a more nuanced or complex understanding of Christ's gospel of peace as one encounters the life stories of people who have suffered from the violence of others and are hungry for revenge.

The humility of respectful dissent requires Christian pacifists to balance several competing considerations. A highly self-conscious sensitivity to other people's points of view can easily become patronizing and condescending. On the other hand, an eagerness to concede points can so diminish the crucial distinctions at stake in conversations about violence that pacifism is reduced to a minor consideration. Dissent, however respectful, is still dissent.

It is also possible that conversations on matters like Christianity and violence will end with neither side moved in any substantive way from their original positions. For the pacifist, however, the lingering questions should always be: did I present my case in a way that consistently reflected Christ's love and compassion, even in the midst of profound disagreements? Have I come to a deeper understanding of the worldview of my conversation partner? Can we leave the exchange with a sense of mutual trust and respect despite our significant differences? The humility of respectful dissent suggests that these considerations may matter as much as the outcome itself.

In every instance, the goal of the Christian pacifist is to give testimony to the joyful path of Christian discipleship. That testimony can be tenacious in its clarity about the truth, even to the point of being willing to suffer and die for it, if necessary. But the gospel of peace is *good* news—a message to be shared with gentleness, integrity, and transparency, not imposed as a burdensome obligation. Humility calls us to listen with care and empathy and to preserve the dignity of others, even when our perspectives in matters as important as faith may differ profoundly.

Each of these various expressions of humility reminds us that Christ's way of peace goes beyond merely avoiding conflict or abstaining from physical violence. In choosing against war, Christian pacifists are embracing a way of life that permeates their entire beings. This way of being in the world, I have suggested, offers a genuine alternative to the powerful temptations in our culture to respond to differences by either imposing our will by force or by retreating into relativism.

> *"Do not be conformed to this world, but be transformed by the renewing of your minds."*
> Romans 12:2

Humility in Action: Hospitality, Honesty, and Humor

You may want to argue that this way of putting things is far too dramatic. Most of our lives are not spent poised at the brink of a decision between lethal violence and disengaged retreat. For most of us, life consists primarily of the far more mundane activities of work, family, recreation, community, and church.

I want to conclude by suggesting that genuine Christian humility—the inner spirit of Christian pacifism—should permeate all of life, the mundane as well as the exceptional. To describe fully how that might look would probably call for an extended discussion of the classic Christian virtues (justice, mercy, fortitude, and prudence) and some reflections on the fruits of the spirit (love, joy, patience, self-control, peace, goodness, faithfulness, kindness, gentleness).

Instead, I want to conclude this chapter by highlighting three specific practices that point toward Christian humility in action. You do not need to be a pacifist to affirm these practices, but I think each of them is indispensable to the worldview of a Christian committed to the gospel of peace.

True Christian humility finds expression in the habits of Hospitality.

Hospitality in our North American setting has generally come to mean hosting the Christmas meal for the extended family or inviting friends over for lunch after church. The biblical theme of hospitality, however, suggests something a bit more radical. Almost always, hospitality in the scriptures refers to the kindness God's people are called to extend, not to their friends, but to strangers—those people we encounter who have no relatives or social network to fall back on in their hour of need.

In the Old Testament, the prophets consistently held up the compassionate treatment of strangers as a crucial measure of the community's faithfulness to God. In the New Testament, Jesus told his disciples that in welcoming the stranger, feeding the hungry, and visiting the sick they were doing acts of kindness to the Son of Man himself (Matthew 10:40-42).

The writer of the book of Hebrews, after reminding the newly established church of the many heroes of the tradition—the familiar anchors of community identity—went on to insist that they should always extend hospitality to those beyond the boundaries of the community: "Do not neglect to show hospitality to strangers," Paul writes, "for by doing that some have entertained angels without knowing it" (Hebrews 13:2).

Susanna Longacre was a Christian pacifist living in Chester County, Pennsylvania, in the early 1780s during the closing years of the American Revolution. The worst years of the war were passed, and rumors were circulating that a peace treaty between the colonists and the British was about to be signed. One spring day in 1783, Susanna's husband, Jacob, was away on business, leaving her in the company of an 8- or 9-year-old girl, perhaps one of her granddaughters. While she worked, Susanna heard a knock at the door. She was used to this sort of interruption, she later said, since her home was located along a well traveled public road to Philadelphia and people often stopped to ask for directions or for something to eat. When she opened the door that fateful morning she saw four tired-looking men. They identified themselves as British soldiers who were hungry, thirsty, and lost. So Susanna did what she always did when the weary stopped by her home—she invited them into the kitchen and set out food and drink. When they had finished, the soldiers thanked her for the food and asked directions to the next town. Susanna saw them to the door, assuming that this was the end of her encounter with them.

But the next day the men reappeared, this time not as British soldiers, but as soldiers of the Revolutionary army who had come to arrest her. In truth, they were American spies traveling about the countryside, trying to expose local farmers who were willing to assist the enemy. The evidence was clear. Susanna was arrested, quickly convicted, and sentenced to pay a heavy fine of £150. Or, if she was unable to pay the fine, the tribunal ordered that she receive 117 lashes "on her bare back at the public post."[1]

Susanna and her husband were distraught. They appealed the sentence as too harsh for a 70-year old woman. Moreover, in her appeal she insisted that she had treated the visitors no differently than any other wayfarers who knocked on her door—her behavior, the petition stated, was "an act of hospitality corresponding with her general conduct for many years past." Indeed, so renowned was Susanna's generosity in the community that 54 of her Lutheran and Reformed neighbors signed a statement in support of her petition.

The historical sources do not record the outcome of the appeal. But it is clear that Susanna Longacre's decision to invite four hungry strangers to eat at her table was not an isolated, or calculated, act of goodness. It was rather part of a much deeper impulse, woven into a long tradition of a faith-based community that refused to allow politics or class or race or religion to define the boundaries of generosity. She had fed the travelers "not because they were British, but because they were hungry."

The biblical virtue of hospitality suggests that Christians are constantly prepared to engage the "Other" in our society, in whatever form that might take, in a posture of open embrace. Hospitality implies a readiness to interrupt our plans on behalf of others, to take a risk of friendship that might not be reciprocated. At an even deeper level, it calls us to consider, even if only for a moment, thoughts and perspectives, theological arguments and political propositions, that are fundamentally at odds with our convictions about the truth.

It might be helpful to ask yourself: who are the persons whose attitudes and opinions I want to change the most? Who stands most in need of my insights about the nature of reality? If you do this honestly, the chances are pretty good that you are defining the Other, the person most in need of your gestures of hospitality. We already know that we have something to teach this person, and perhaps appropriately so. But is there anything that we might also have to learn from such people? Would we be willing to go the second mile to create and defend space so that this person's perspectives might be heard?

In the habits of hospitality, pacifism becomes embodied within the routines of daily life.

True Christian humility finds expression in the habits of Honesty. On the surface, an appeal to honesty sounds rather bland. After all, would anyone really advocate anything else? Why would this be a distinctive characteristic of the pacifist Christian? In a culture that tends to affirm an openness to every claim to truth, however, the practice of honesty is actually a very radical gesture, especially if it is woven into the practice of hospitality.

Honesty compels Christians to make moral and ethical distinctions, to name injustices and to confront wrongdoings, regardless of whether they are present in our families, our congregations, our communities, or the larger culture. Cultivating the practice of honesty requires both courage and integrity. It assumes a confidence in our understanding of the truth that is not easily swayed by threats or flattery, and it demands consistency between our words and our actions. The practice of honesty may lead us in unsettling directions. It may call us to a kind of holy unrest in which we challenge the status quo and refuse to remain silent in the face of what we know to be wrong.

If we truly believe that God is the one who calls us to the way of peace, then we should not hesitate to give verbal expression to our commitments. At the same time, however, the honesty that may lead to confrontation and disagreement never does so at the expense of the unconditional embrace of hospitality.

In 1553 a Christian pacifist and reformer named Menno Simons was active in the north German city of Wismar.

The city had recently issued a very sharp edict against Menno and his group of religious dissenters, the Anabaptists. So he and his small congregation in Wismar were forced to meet in secret.

Coincidentally, that same year another group of religious dissidents—some Calvinists living in England—had also come under the shadow of religious persecution and were forced by Queen Mary to flee England in the dead of winter. The group of beleaguered religious refugees reached the harbor of Wismar in December of 1553. But Wismar was a Lutheran city and the town magistrates had made it clear that they were not interested in permitting these Reformed believers to settle in the town. There, anchored some distance away from the shore, the ship froze fast in the ice, putting the lives of its passengers in jeopardy.

When Menno and the secret Anabaptist congregation of Wismar heard of the refugees, however, they quietly organized a relief party to bring them to shore and supplied them with food throughout the rest of the winter.

The point of the story might have been the generous gesture of hospitality. But there is another layer to the encounter that bears closer attention. As it turned out, the two groups disagreed with each other sharply on various points of doctrine. Eventually, the leader of the Calvinist group called in a theologian from the nearby city of Emden to debate Menno on various understandings of faith. The outcome of that debate only further underscored the differences between the two groups.

Indeed, through the encounter both sides were pushed to clarify their positions with new rigor and precision. Yet the crucial point is that this kind of honest and frank exchange could happen without ever calling into question whether the Anabaptist congregation had done the right thing in extending aid to vulnerable strangers in their midst, even though these strangers turned out to be theologically far apart from them.

And finally, true Christian humility finds expression in the habits of Humor.

Analysis and debate over ethical questions can easily become very heavy. The dangerous thing about dealing with serious matters is that we can start to take ourselves far too seriously— and become consumed by the burdens and complexities of our issues.

When, in the computer lingo of our times, we threaten to lock up emotionally or mentally, humor is a kind of spiritual reset button offering a way out of the impasse. The power of humor lies precisely in its element of surprise. A joke is funny because it leads us along the path of the familiar and then suddenly, out of the blue, takes us to unexpected territory. In the moment of that mental free fall, when we let go of our assumptions and suddenly see the outcome in a whole new way, we respond with laughter.

To be sure, humor can be dangerous. Some people can take offense when their deeply held beliefs are pushed into a free fall or when they personally are made the brunt of a joke. Humor can become vicious if it only reinforces stereotypes. Satire is risky.

But the best humor generates shared experiences of momentary weightlessness in which we see our common foibles, laugh at our assumptions, and come back to the world of reality with a healthier perspective on our shared limits and possibilities. At its best, the surprising twist of humor reminds us that even our most serious convictions should be held lightly, that a divine perspective is ultimately always bigger than our grasp of the truth.

Conclusion

One of the biggest challenges in our culture today is to negotiate the chasm between a rampant relativism incapable of making moral judgments and absolutist claims about truth that are intolerant of any dissent. In this chapter, I have suggested that a Christian commitment to nonviolence, anchored in humility, offers an alternative to the narrow options of "fight or flight."

At their best, Christians are called to be both bold and tentative in their witness. In word and deed they will testify without hesitation to the reality of God's presence in the world; yet at the same time they will speak that truth in a spirit of gentleness and love, never allowing their understanding of God's will to become a weapon of manipulation or coercion.

This position of confident humility is not easy to maintain. It is not a static position, but a dynamic, unfolding mystery into which one lives each day—rooted in the disciplines of prayer, the active discernment of scripture, and regular confession. It is a path shaped by the daily practices of hospitality, honesty, and humor. It is a journey to be undertaken only in the company of other believers, whose counsel and encouragement help us maintain perspective when we are overwhelmed by the difficulty of the challenge.

But, perhaps most important, it is also a journey of deep joy, sustained by God's presence and grace, in which each day holds the possibility of a new adventure and the promise of Shalom.

---

[1] Richard MacMaster, et al., eds. *Conscience in Crisis* (Scottdale, PA: Herald Press, 1979), 515-516.

5.

"IN GOD WE TRUST"— THE DILEMMAS OF CHRISTIAN CITIZENSHIP

"In Christ there is no East or West,
In Him no South or North;
But one great fellowship of love
Throughout the whole wide earth."

William A. Dunkerley, 1908

O n July 30, 1956, President Eisenhower signed into law a congressional resolution that made the phrase "In God We Trust" the official motto of the United States. Only a year previous, on June 11, 1955, Eisenhower had endorsed a similar bill making it mandatory for all U.S. coins and paper currency to bear the same inscription: "In God We Trust." Both laws were passed at the height of the McCarthy era, amid concern that godless communism was on the march at home and abroad. They reflected widespread sentiment in the United States that the political fate of the country was directly linked to God's blessing and favor. While a few may have lamented the retirement of *E pluribus unum* (Out of many, one) or chafed at the religious overtones of the new motto, Congress passed the resolution by a very wide margin, and the action seemed relatively uncontroversial. The phrase "In God We Trust" reminded Americans of the common faith shared by the country's founders, and it hinted strongly at a special relationship between God and the American people, a relationship in which trust would be rewarded by divine favor.

For most Americans the phrase "In God We Trust" does not merit a second thought. So deeply is the motto engrained in the bedrock of American identity that few are inclined to take it all that seriously. Yet our familiarity with the phrase should not obscure the revolutionary nature of its claim. Whether we think about it consciously or not, our national motto makes a clear statement about our deepest allegiances and our ultimate loyalties—it is a religious confession of faith that has profound political consequences. For in claiming it, we are affirming with

> *"For there is no distinction between Jew and Greek; the same Lord is Lord of all and generous to all who call on Him . . ."*
> Romans 10:12

Christians around the world and throughout the ages that our final security is found not in the nation itself, but in the God of Abraham and the church of Jesus Christ.

Thus, it is both confusing and potentially dangerous for Christians to link the words "In God We Trust" with the symbols of national identity. However benign our intentions may be, the biblical admonition to put our trust completely in God can very easily come into tension with claims that compete for our trust and allegiance, especially those wrapped in patriotic symbols calling us to put national identity above all else.

In this chapter I want to explore more deeply what it means to proclaim that our trust is in God, especially in the context of modern citizenship and the subtle appeal of patriotism. Christians, I suggest, are citizens of not one, but two, kingdoms: that of the nation state and that of the universal body of Christ. As citizens of the country we carry passports, obey the local laws and acknowledge the authority of our rulers. But the Christian's *primary* citizenship is in the church of Jesus Christ, the gathering of Christ's followers that transcends national boundaries.

United by a common Master, sharing the free gift of God's grace, Christians should proclaim Christ's love in everything they do, even when that commitment brings them into conflict with the interests of the state. For ultimately our trust is in *God*, not in the nation.

Trust in God

Few themes resound more clearly or consistently in the biblical story than the admonition to "trust in God." From Genesis to Revelation, the people of God are repeatedly confronted with a choice regarding their loyalty: will they put their trust in God or will they turn their allegiances elsewhere?

The Old Testament narratives are filled with stories in which the Children of Israel were put to the test on this question. And frequently they came up wanting. Against God's wishes, for example, the Israelites elected a king so that they could "be like other nations" (I Samuel 8:20). Time and again, God warned the Children of Israel against putting their faith in chariots of steel (Psalm 20:7) or in princes (Psalm 146:3) or in fortified cities (Jeremiah 5:17) or in riches (Jeremiah 49:4; Proverbs 11:28) or in false gods (Jeremiah 13:25), rather than trusting in Him alone. Even after God provided a miraculous escape from Egypt and promised them a land "flowing with milk and honey," the Children of Israel wavered in their allegiance and, while Moses was absent, began to worship a golden calf (Exodus 32:1-6). Indeed, the entire history of God's people in the Old Testament teeters on this question of trust.

The theme continues to echo in the New Testament as well. Over and over again, Jesus called on his disciples to put their security in God rather than in money or status or power. Paul repeatedly admonished the newly established churches to direct their loyalty to Christ alone. And the story of the early church is filled with stirring accounts of people whose resolute faith in Christ and trust in God was so deep that it led to their persecution and death.

On this basic point, the scriptural record is clear. It is God, not humans, who knows the future and directs the course of history. God is a "jealous God" who asks that His people live vulnerably, trusting completely in His power and strength.

Trust in God is always a choice made in a context of tempting and compelling alternatives. And since these alternative claims on our allegiance can assume so many different guises, our choice to trust in God must be renewed every day.

How ironic then that the phrase "In God We Trust" would appear, of all places, on our money, especially since Jesus was painfully explicit to his followers that they could not "serve God and wealth" (Luke 16:13). But even though wealth poses one of the most obvious detractions from our trust in God alone, it is certainly not the only competing claim to our allegiance.

Consider, for example, some of the other symbols of power and allegiance depicted on a simple one-dollar bill alongside the motto "In God We Trust." The dollar's front side, of course, bears the familiar image of George Washington. Hero of the Revolutionary War and the embodiment of national virtue, Washington reminds citizens that patriotic loyalty to their country can entail sacrifice, especially in times of war. On the back side of the dollar bill, the motto "In God We Trust" is flanked on the left by symbols of the Enlightenment and Reason: an Egyptian pyramid, peaked with the all-seeing eye of a rational God and encircled by the Latin phrases "a new order of the ages" (*novus ordo seclorum*) and "God favors our undertakings" (*annuit coeptis*).

> *"Peter and the apostles answered, 'We must obey God rather than any human authority.'"*
>
> Acts 5:29

To the right appears the American eagle, a fierce symbol of national power and pride. Significantly, the eagle's talons hold both the olive branch of peace and a clutch of arrows, conveying a clear message: the security Americans enjoy in times of peace can be guaranteed only if we are ready to defend that peace with the armaments of war.

Thus, if you look at a dollar bill more closely, the national motto "In God We Trust" turns out to be juxtaposed with several other competing claims on our loyalty—money, patriotic ideals, the power of reason, and the strength of a national army.

The point of all this is not to suggest that these other sources of authority in our lives are inherently bad. Money, after all, is crucial for the exchange of goods and services; political heroes can inspire us to sacrificial and charitable deeds; reason is the foundation of civil public discourse; and the social stability secured by the government's coercive authority is far superior to the alternatives of chaos and anarchy. These competing symbols of allegiance and trust are not intrinsically evil. But their appearance alongside the Christian confession that it is "In *God* We Trust" raises a host of important questions that merit closer attention.

In our own context, Christians tend to be aware of the potential seductions of wealth. Many believers also readily acknowledge that human reason can become a substitute for faith in God. But North American Christians are generally far less suspicious of patriotism and national allegiance as competitors for our trust in God. Indeed, many Christians would be surprised to think that faith in Christ or membership in his church could ever be at odds with their loyalty to the nation, so sure are they that patriotic citizenship and faithful Christianity are one and the same thing. Yet I wish to suggest that the biblical message to trust in God and our commitment as members of the church of Jesus Christ will *inevitably* be in tension with our patriotic allegiance to the nation.

In the following section, I want to illustrate the conflict between our claims to trust in God and the obligations of patriotic citizenship by looking at three areas of possible tension: (1) the symbols and rituals of patriotism; (2) the language that identifies America as a "Christian nation;" and (3) the call of our leaders in times of war to kill on behalf of the country.

In each of these areas, I suggest that Christians' profession of trust in God should redefine the nature of their allegiance to the nation-state. The concluding section of the chapter anticipates several questions that are frequently addressed to Christian pacifists by those who are disturbed by the apparent consequences of my call for a more qualified form of patriotism.

If many of the points made in this chapter are somewhat critical of deeply rooted convictions regarding patriotism and political responsibility, I hope readers will continue to the following chapter. There I develop a more positive case for civic engagement and suggest alternative ways in which committed Christian pacifists are giving creative, transformative, and relevant expression to their faith.

Should Christians Be Patriotic?

"In God We Trust." For many Christian Americans, expressions of patriotic sentiments are organically fused with their understanding of responsible, God-fearing citizenship. Of course Christians should be patriotic. After all, patriotism celebrates the freedoms of speech and religion that make it possible to worship God freely in this country.

Patriotism honors the sacrifices previous generations have made to ensure those freedoms. Patriotism binds a potentially splintered constellation of racial and ethnic groups, religious denominations, political parties, and other special interests into a unified nation. It inspires us to heroic deeds of valor and courage. Why would Christians want to be skeptical about the sentiments and symbols of these virtues?

It may be helpful to begin by distinguishing among various forms of patriotic sentiment. Certainly the regional pride residents of the Pacific Northwest often express in the natural beauty of their home states is hardly a threat to Christian identity or trust in God. A deep appreciation for the folkways and rich history of one's native country need not be in sharp tension with commitments to God or to Christ's church. The concerns about patriotism I wish to raise here are not intended to belittle the love and commitment that many Christians have for their country or to imply a disdain for such songs as "America, the Beautiful."

At the same time, however, appeals to our patriotic sentiments, especially in times of war, can easily become a direct challenge to the trust that Christians say is due to God alone. After all, patriotism, like faith, celebrates a sense of belonging to a group and a destiny larger than ourselves. Like faith, patriotism is less a matter of the mind than of the heart and soul. It appeals to our emotions, it tugs on our heartstrings, it evokes deep sentiments of nostalgia and a longing for security. Precisely because patriotic impulses are so subtle and powerful, Christians should be thoughtful about patriotism's potential to usurp the trust and security that we claim is reserved for God.

Patriotism—or "love for the fatherland" (*patria*)—is an ancient concept, going back at least as far as the Greek city-state or the Roman republic. But the modern form of patriotism we know today was forged in the fires of the American and French revolutions and deeply shaped by the new model of participatory democracy that those revolutions fought to establish.

For most of European history, political loyalty was highly personal in nature. Feudal allegiances—that of a vassal to a lord, for example, or a subject to a king—were sealed by face-to-face oaths of fealty and homage. Subjects could petition their sovereigns in the manner of a child before a stern parent in the hopes of gaining some particular exemption or a unique privilege. But the bonds of loyalty were generally focused on an individual rather than an abstract political entity.

The American and French revolutions fundamentally reconceived the nature of political allegiances. As democracies promising rights and liberties to all of their citizens and guaranteeing equality under the law, these new states faced the profound challenge of political unity. Absent a king, what would unite the divisive mix of rich and poor, noble and peasant, Catholic and Protestant into a coherent civic order?

The solution was the emergence of a new form of patriotism. Whereas the older notion of patriotism implied simply a "love of the fatherland," patriotism in the modern era required the conscious, systematic cultivation of allegiance to the symbols of national unity, often sanctioned by religious language that fused loyalty to the nation with the promise of God's special blessing.

This new form of patriotism was much more explicitly militaristic in tone. Conscripted citizen militias replaced mercenary armies. And these new "people's armies"—unified by parades, flags, uniforms, patriotic speeches, and benedictory prayers—fought now not for the king, or even national borders, but for the transcendent cause of the nation's ideals and principles. Such was the price of equality under the law and the right to full participation in the political process.

Thus, for most of modern history, patriotism has served as a kind of social glue unifying its citizens around the ideals of freedom and democracy, but always with the reminder that these ideals will require its citizens to die (and to kill) whenever the nation is at war. Patriotism in the U.S. context is inextricably linked to the battlefield.

At a deep emotional level, arguments for patriotism, and our practical experience with the symbols of nationhood, often "feel" right. They appeal both to positive sentiments and to deeply held principles. When we see the flag unfurling in a gentle breeze or sing the "Star Spangled Banner" or say the Pledge of Allegiance or join in the pageantry of a Fourth of July parade, we find ourselves caught up in a sense of pride and loyalty and power that bonds us to the nation.

But the subtle and cumulative effect of patriotic sentiments is to nurture a deep, primal loyalty to the nation and its leaders that in times of crisis can very quickly trump our claims to trust in God or our bonds of fellowship with Christians in the worldwide church of Jesus Christ.

When we repeat the Pledge of Allegiance with our hands over our hearts, or when we stand with thousands of others before a sporting event to sing the national anthem, or when we prominently display flags from our porches, we are giving public testimony to our loyalty. If not stating so explicitly, we are certainly implying that the nation can count on us to defend it—to kill on its behalf—in times of war. Patriotic emotions lead us to believe that the principles embodied in our nation are, like God, actually transcendent and therefore worthy of the ultimate sacrifice entailed by killing and dying in their defense.

At the very least, Christians should pause to ask how such symbols and assumptions mesh with their repeated claim to trust in God, especially against the backdrop of the biblical story in which idolatry—that is, trust in something other than God—was such a persistent and troubling temptation. Are Christians really trusting in God when they support their troops in times of war? Or are we simply reshaping God into our own national image, making Him into a tribal deity who will simply bless whatever actions we choose to take? Can the flag become a golden calf, tempting us to put our trust in things made by human hands rather than in the God of the universe?

Does the Christian's response to the patriotic demands of the nation differ in any significant way from the response non-Christians might give? If, as many Christians would insist, our commitments to Christ do indeed ultimately trump the authority of the nation, then by what criteria would Christians know when the claims of the nation have intruded on the integrity of the gospel?

In a similar vein, Christians should think more carefully about the meaning of patriotic allegiances in light of the international body of Christians. Should, for example, those believers living in Canada or Zambia or China or Saudi Arabia be pledging allegiance to *their* nations as well, promising to die in defense of *their* national ideals and borders?

If we Christians in North America truly wish to claim the national motto "In God We Trust," then let us be honest about the subtle ways in which patriotism redirects our trust away from God to the nation, to its leaders, to military might, and to our own self-interest.

Is There Such a Thing as a "Christian Nation"?

"In God We Trust." For many American Christians, it is almost blasphemous to ask whether or not America is a Christian nation. Of course we are, they say. Or, if we have not yet fully reached that status, we should at least *aspire* to become a Christian nation. After all, this country was founded on Christian principles. Our Pledge of Allegiance states that we are "one nation under God," they add.

The great majority of our political leaders have professed to be Christians, many citing a personal experience of being "born again." In times of national crisis our presidents routinely call us to prayer. In many Protestant churches the Stars and Stripes are prominently displayed alongside the Christian flag. When we sing "God Bless America" we do so with the assumption that we are already a nation truly worthy of God's special favor.

To be sure, a stubborn minority has always challenged these efforts to identify America as a Christian nation. But these have generally been the scattered voices of legal scholars concerned about the separation of church and state, or small minority groups worried about their fate under a theocracy, or historians quibbling about whether the Deism of Thomas Jefferson can be equated with the Christianity of the Moral Majority.

Yet the Christian community itself, the very group that should be raising the most powerful arguments against the idea of a Christian nation, has largely maintained a deafening silence on the issue. Indeed, Christians have often been among the most aggressive promoters of the concept, despite the seductive nature of the claim that threatens to undermine the very integrity of the Christian church.

New Testament believers will note that the concept of a Christian nation is completely absent from the gospel or its proclamation by the apostles and the early church. The only biblical example of a political entity uniquely associated with God's will and purpose was that of Israel in the Old Testament, the descendants of Abraham whom God promised to make into "a great nation" (Genesis 12:2). But even in the case of the Children of Israel, scriptures make it clear that their primary identity as a people was defined by their *trust in God* and explicitly *not* in the strength of their armies, the power of their kings, or even the boundaries of their territory.

Indeed, it was precisely the symbols of national identity and pride that made it so difficult for Israel to remain dependent on God. And yet when Israel as a political entity ceased to exist, as it did during the period of exile when the armies of Assyria and Babylon had swallowed up all of Palestine, Israel's identity as a people of God endured. Why? Not because they had successfully defended their borders, but because—even in their moment of exile and vulnerability—they reaffirmed their commitment to serve God and God alone.

This surprising, counterintuitive approach to trust and collective identity became the centerpiece of the liberating message of the Gospel. No longer are God's followers to be defined in terms of race or ethnicity, political loyalties or national citizenship. No! In the person of Jesus Christ, God's invitation to Shalom is now extended to *all* people. In the familiar words of John 3:16 we read that God gave His only Son for the *entire world*—not for any particular people or nation. In Christ, wrote Paul, "there is no longer Jew or Greek, there is no longer slave or free, male and female . . . ." (Galatians 3:28). And in his tireless missionary journeys to the Gentiles, Paul offered dramatic proof that the gospel of Christ and his church transcended boundaries of geography and politics.

Throughout the whole of the New Testament, God's work of redemption is always presented as being universal in scope. That redemptive action took on tangible form not in the political structures of the Roman Empire, but in the church, the gathered body of Christ's disciples who rejected the claims of Caesar's lordship and united themselves around the proclamation that "Jesus is Lord!" In a very real sense, the church is its own "holy nation," in the language of I Peter (2:9), "God's own people," a social and political reality wherever two or three are gathered in Christ's name, that assumes its own concrete form distinct from the nation.

The idea that a territory defined by geographic boundaries could somehow be defined as Christian is theologically incoherent and idolatrous. What specific theological or ethical criteria, after all, would qualify a nation to claim the label of "Christian"? Does it mean that 51% or more of its citizens consider themselves Christians? Does it imply that all of its leaders are Christians? Does it mean that the nation's constitution and laws are distilled directly from the Bible? Or that such biblically based laws should be righteously enforced—in jihad-like fashion, with divine authority—on all citizens?

If the New Testament is to be relevant for our legal code and political culture, then shouldn't Christians be lobbying all elected and appointed leaders, including those in the Department of Defense and Pentagon officials, to live in accordance with the clear teachings of Jesus in the Sermon on the Mount?

To be sure, a sovereign God remains Lord over all of creation, including the nations of the earth. God exercises His will in and through the nations, often in ways that we cannot fully understand. But this important theological observation should not detract from the fact that the *primary* arena for God's saving work in the world is the church, the body of believers gathered in the name of the resurrected Christ. After all, when Christ returns, he will come to claim the church as his bride, not the nation.

Christians whose primary identity is anchored in their national citizenship rather than in their allegiance to the body of Christ should ask some hard questions about the nature of their faith. Since the coming of Christ, God's gift of forgiveness and the call to become disciples of Jesus have always been invitations to individuals, not to nations. And it is the living body of Christ, the church—not the nation—where God continues to be revealed most fully to the world.

If Christians in America truly wish to claim the motto "In God We Trust" with integrity, then we should be very skeptical about the assumption that America, or any other country, is indeed a Christian Nation.

Should Christians Participate in Wars?

"In God We Trust." Asking whether or not Christians should serve in the armed forces may strike many Christians as preposterous as questioning patriotism or casting doubts on the notion of a Christian Nation. Of course Christians should serve in the military! As residents of a free country, Christians are obliged no less than all other citizens to defend the boundaries of our country and the principles of "life, liberty, and the pursuit of happiness" for which our country stands.

Naturally, nobody is eager to die in battle, but the responsibilities of citizenship are not something that you can simply claim or reject at your own discretion. If you enjoy the benefits of living in a country ruled by law and based on the principles of liberty, then you should be ready to sacrifice on its behalf, even if it may mean killing others or giving your life in the line of duty.

For some readers these arguments are so transparently obvious that it may be tempting to stop right here. But throughout the sweep of church history, a small group of Christians has consistently witnessed to the fact that the love of Christ extends to *all* human beings—including enemies. Such convictions have often brought with them great cost and personal sacrifice. These Christians have not intended their witness to be disrespectful to those in authority nor to imply a disregard for the painful losses many families have endured as a result of combat. Instead, Christian pacifists are simply enacting their allegiance to a Lord who has renounced violence and has modeled for his disciples the paradoxical power of a love that is stronger than our fear.

In order to understand more deeply why Christians might hold such convictions—especially in the face of enormous pressure to conform—we must begin by emphasizing the genuine *choice* that lies at the heart of this crucial question. In matters bearing on participation in war or the taking of human life, every individual must reflect deeply on his or her convictions and come to a conscious decision about the rationale for the actions that follow.

Taking conscious responsibility for our choices in these matters is actually much harder than it may seem. Frequently in life we find ourselves doing things that we actually choose to do, but without fully realizing that we made a choice. Impulse shopping at the mall, an overly full schedule of appointments, a maxed-out credit card, a lonely weekend—all these are consequences of specific decisions that somehow never felt like a decision at the time.

The same is true with our choices regarding military participation and support for our nation's wars. Our culture is suffused with stories of national heroes, symbols of national pride, statues and plaques commemorating those who have died in wars, and sophisticated military recruitment campaigns that are all designed to encourage support for the nation's war effort as an obvious, honorable, and maybe even inevitable consequence of being an American citizen.

Often these cultural encouragements to support the military are powerfully reinforced by the religious community which promises young people in the armed forces the full blessing of God and the church. Many Christian congregations are as proud of their young people in the military as they are of those members who are serving as missionaries.

The cumulative effect of all of this is to make it seem as if supporting your country in war is not really an individual decision, but the inevitable outcome of common sense, patriotic allegiance, and the will of God. Such is the power of a worldview.

However, if we assume that the question of participation in war is indeed a *choice* rather than a foregone conclusion, what might be some of the crucial considerations that have a bearing on that decision? Here again we meet up with the fundamental issue of trust and identity.

I have suggested in earlier chapters that God yearns for humans to live with each other in vulnerability, compassion, and intimacy. This is the goal of Shalom for which we were originally created. This ideal of human fulfillment is captured most concretely in the life and teachings of Jesus. In Christ we have been saved from sin and the fallen order of the world into salvation and the new order of creation that God is establishing in the church.

As believers, then, our trust and security will be focused primarily on Christ and the church, not on ties and commitments that promise security for those in the natural world. Jesus put it most bluntly when he told his disciples that they could not serve two masters: "for a slave will either hate the one and love the other, or be devoted to the one and despise the other" (Matthew 6:24).

To be sure, Christ is no longer physically present in the world, and some Christians have rejected this call for a more radical form of allegiance as irrelevant for those today who are not living in the physical presence of Jesus. But many other Christians would testify that Christ remains alive in the world, both through the Holy Spirit and, more concretely, in the social reality of the Christian church—the so-called "Body of Christ."

The contemporary Christian church, like its members, is not perfect. Far from it! But it stands within the flow of history as a concrete testimony to the radically new kingdom that Jesus inaugurated, and it points toward the fulfillment of time when the reign of Christ will restore all of creation. For Christians who are living between Christ's resurrection and the end of time, the church is the primary point of reference for Christ's living presence in the world.

This does not mean that Christians must reject culture, society, and politics altogether. In a fallen and chaotic world, those human institutions that bring order and jus-

> "Because Jesus commanded his followers to love their enemies and then died as the incarnate Son to demonstrate that God reconciles His enemies by suffering love, any rejection of the nonviolent way in human relations involves a heretical doctrine of the atonement."
>
> Ron Sider, *Christ and Violence*, 34

tice do, at least, point in the direction of Shalom. But when it comes to decisions as fundamental as taking the life of another person to defend these human institutions and ideals; or when it comes to the question of whether we will consciously prepare ourselves to intimidate, threaten, maim, and kill other human beings; or when we have the clear choice of participating in an institution whose members are trained to obey orders without question, then Christians are facing fundamental issues of trust and security that go to the heart of their deepest commitments.

It is at this point, I believe, that we Christians must ask which master we will serve: the call of Christ to drop our nets and follow him in vulnerability, or the call of the nation to pick up our weapons, march to its drumbeat, and kill those who threaten our interests.

As in the first century, there are many different understandings of Christ and the gospel today. Yet, like Peter, we must be prepared to offer an answer when Jesus asks, what about you? Who do you say that I am? Can we say with Peter, "You are the Christ, the Son of the Living God"; the bringer of Shalom, the healer of the nations, the Prince of Peace whose death on the cross and resurrection in glory is the means of our salvation and the model for our lives.

OK . . . But I Still Have Some Questions!

You may be thinking at this point that perhaps Christians should indeed be more cautious about embracing the symbols and rituals of patriotism, that perhaps it would be best if Christians looked to the church more than the nation as the primary focus of God's presence in the world, that perhaps followers of Christ should be hesitant about following the call of the nation to war. But all of these affirmations raise many other vexing questions.

For example, even if you were willing to renounce violence in self-defense, don't Christians *still* have some responsibility for the welfare and protection of their fellow human beings? Aren't there times when the quest for moral purity can actually become selfish, especially if it means that innocent people might suffer because of your convictions? Might there be circumstances in which the truly loving response would be to renounce your abstract principles, no matter how high-minded, so that the lives of real people could be saved? In the end, some people have argued, pacifism seems less heroic than egotistical—an evasion of social obligations in the interests of maintaining some Olympian standard of moral purity.

These are important questions, ones that Christian pacifists have not always taken as seriously as they should. No pacifist, least of all a Christian pacifist, should turn her or his back on human suffering in the face of violence. Indeed, as I will suggest in Chapter Six, Christian pacifists are called by their vision of Shalom to engage the fallen world actively and creatively, not to run from it. But in our haste to defend circumstances in which violence seems to be the only acceptable recourse, we can very easily rationalize our impulse to power and control in ways that are really closer to a Nitzschean than a Christian worldview.

Let us consider some of the questions that are frequently posed to Christian pacifists and, in the spirit of humility outlined in Chapter Four, offer a response and a counter-challenge in defense of Christ's way of peace.

What would you do if . . . ?

Probably no question is put to Christian pacifists more frequently, or with more imaginative detail, than some variation on the classic query: "what would you do if someone was threatening to kill your wife and children and the only way to stop him was to shoot him—to use lethal violence?"

The energy behind the question usually comes from a strong suspicion that pacifists arrive at their convictions in the comfort of some secure setting and in the safe realm of idealistic abstractions. But if pacifists were actually put into dangerous circumstances where they had a highly personal interest at stake, then their lofty principles would quickly evaporate into thin air and common sense would prevail. The details of the hypothetical question may vary, but the essential elements are always the same: unless you eventually are willing to kill, you will be morally responsible for the suffering—maybe even death—of innocent people.

Christian pacifists will undoubtedly answer this question in various ways. As I have reflected on the question in casual conversations on airplanes, in focused debates with colleagues, and in discussions at home and at church, my response usually includes elements of the following:

a. I don't know how I would respond. The truth of the matter is that none of us can know with absolute certainty how we would react in the face of a sudden, dramatic threat to our own lives or the lives of those we love. But this honest confession of uncertainty simply underscores the importance of giving careful thought to our response in advance of the moment, and to preparing ourselves as best we can to do what is *right* rather than merely what our natural impulse might be.

Just as we teach teenagers that they should give careful thought to matters of sexual morality *before* they find themselves in the back seat of a car with their hormones racing, so too Christians ought to reflect carefully on questions of personal violence in anticipation of a moment of crisis. In the end, we don't know exactly how we will respond. But we do have a framework in the life and teaching of Christ for knowing how we should answer the question, and as Christians we should commit ourselves in advance to shaping our response around Christ's example.

b. The question's direct appeal to human nature—to our natural impulse to self-defense and the bonds of affection that connect us with our families—heightens the drama of the moral decision. But few Christians would regard appeals to human nature as an adequate foundation for discerning God's will in matters of ethical decision-making. Simply because our *instincts* are to kill the attacker does not in any way make that choice obviously Christian. Again, consider the example of sexual morality. It is possible that despite all proactive teaching and careful modeling our children will make wrong choices in the heat of sexual desire. But that possibility—understandable though it may be as a natural, human impulse—should not imply that God intended men and women to be sexually intimate apart from marriage.

After all, it is precisely the realities of human nature that make ethical discernment necessary in the first place. Certainly the impulse to use lethal violence is understandable; human nature would urge us to defend ourselves and our loved ones at all costs. But Christians are called to a higher standard of morality than simply conforming to our natural impulses.

c. The theoretical question that begins "what would you do if . . ." is riddled with numerous hidden assumptions about unknown factors that make the question almost empty of meaning. In the way it is usually posed, the question imagines only two possible outcomes: either you kill the attacker, or the attacker kills your loved ones. Yet in real life, the scenario actually could play itself out in many other variations that are almost never considered in the standard framing of the story.

If, for example, you had the right training and fast reflexes, perhaps you could disarm the attacker without killing him. If you were psychologically astute and sufficiently empathetic and gifted in speech, perhaps you could persuade the attacker to give up peacefully. If you had sufficient faith, perhaps God would intervene miraculously. If you shot and missed, perhaps the attacker would end up killing both you and your loved ones. If you shot and killed the attacker, perhaps you would be filled with so much remorse that you would renounce your faith, become an alcoholic, and live the rest of your life in misery. If your loved ones are Christian believers, then you know that they would enjoy eternity in heaven; by killing the attacker (who is presumably not a Christian) you would foreclose forever the possibility that this person would come to know Christ.

The point in playing out these many alternative scenarios is not to argue that any one is more likely to occur than another. But it does suggest that the hypothetical question so frequently posed to pacifists turns out to be far less straightforward than it initially may appear. In general, the question seems designed from the outset to direct the correct answer away from costly forms of discipleship toward a defense of our natural instincts.

d. In the end, I—like all Christian pacifists—am committed not to take the life of another human being, regardless of the consequences. If someone were to attack me or a loved one, I trust that God would give me the courage to find creative, non-lethal ways of resisting that attack. But in the end, I am willing to allow the attacker to kill me and the people I love rather than to shed another person's blood to defend my interests. As an undeserving recipient of God's gracious love, I am called to bear witness to that same love in everything I do, trusting in the power of the resurrection and the hope of eternal life.

Aren't Christian pacifists socially irresponsible?

Some people have argued that pacifists have abandoned all sense of social responsibility. By abstaining from the messy compromises of violence and the rough-and-tumble realities of national defense, Christian pacifists are simply conceding power to those who are truly immoral, or at least to those who care only about advancing their own self-interests. To do this—to allow evil to fill the vacuum of power left by the pacifist—is socially irresponsible.

The charge is a serious one and worthy of closer reflection. The rejection of pacifism on the grounds of social responsibility generally assumes that the nature of our obligations to the state (or to our family, our community, or our neighbor) is simple and straightforward. More importantly, the argument assumes that a responsible action will always keep open the option of using violence. On closer inspection, however, it would seem that both of these assumptions are flawed.

In the first place, the argument for social responsibility is deceptive in that it suggests from the outset that acting "responsibly," that is, using violence to defend the innocent, will inevitably resolve the problem, whereas a commitment to nonviolence will inevitably lead to greater suffering. In some instances this logic may indeed be true. It is possible that a pacifist response to violence could result in the death of innocent people.

But Christian pacifism does not claim to be a political strategy offering any guarantees about the outcome of a given encounter. Its primary goal is not effectiveness in terms of a rationally calculated outcome, but rather faithfulness to the witness of Christ and God's restoration of Shalom.

That said, however, the death of innocent people is by no means an inevitable or self-evident outcome of nonviolent action. Certainly the examples in recent history of the Solidarity movement in Poland, the so-called Velvet Revolution in Czechoslovakia (1989), People Power in the Philippines (1986), or the largely nonviolent resistance to communism in East Germany and other eastern bloc countries, all of which offer evidence that pacifism in those circumstances—even in the face of grave injustice and powerful military threats—was actually a more socially responsible approach to political transformation than the violent impulses of the reactionary or the revolutionary.

Second, the implication that the truly responsible option in social ethics is inherently clear simply does not square with reality. All people, and perhaps especially Christians, have a deep sense of responsibility to fulfill their various duties as parents, workers, citizens, and believers. But the exact nature of these responsibilities is often shaped by the context and circumstances within which they emerge. Responsibilities are never crystal clear or self-evident. And precisely because we have multiple responsibilities (to our children, our bosses, our communities, our churches, etc.), we are constantly faced with the challenge of balancing and choosing priorities among the competing demands these obligations place on our time, money, and energy.

Any parent will immediately recognize the tension involved when our responsibility for providing for our families conflicts with our responsibility for spending time with our children, or our responsibility for nurturing our marriage relationship, or for being actively involved in civic affairs, or for supporting the work of the church. These struggles between competing obligations are a given in modern life. Every day we are forced to make difficult choices—ideally in accordance with our principles and convictions—about the meaning and nature of our responsibilities. So we ask ourselves such questions as: responsible to whom (my family? the state? the world? God?), and responsible for what (to ensure security? to make money? to preserve life? to be faithful to the teachings of Christ?)?

Our political or social responsibilities to the country are no different. Here, just as in many other areas of life, we choose among alternative possibilities in ways that reflect our deepest commitments. If one begins with a clear commitment to Shalom and a conviction that ultimately God is the guarantor of our security, then nonviolence may actually be the most responsible course of action.

In any event, the apparent dilemmas of social responsibility are no different for us than for Jesus himself. At the very beginning of his ministry, Jesus faced powerful forces within the Jewish community that tried to push him into a quite specific understanding of his responsibilities as a Jew. The Zealots, for example, had a clear vision of a restored Israel based on a military insurrection and their political liberation from the Roman oppressors. The Pharisees were deeply offended that Jesus did not adopt a responsible attitude toward a strict observance of the Law. The Sadducees found his agitation among lower class Jews socially irresponsible in light of the conservative order they were trying to preserve. And the Essenes understood the only responsible option to be a retreat from the whole scene into the monastic purity of the desert.

Like Jesus, Christians will inevitably face competing definitions of social responsibility. And, like Jesus, the Christian pacifist's choice of an upside-down approach to security, one based on the vulnerable power of love, will likely offend some and leave others deeply disappointed.

Yet in the end, Jesus refused to allow his own sense of mission and purpose to be defined by conventional understandings of what was socially responsible. His pursuit of a higher calling and purpose, always in service to Shalom, disrupted standard assumptions and challenged those who followed him to consider a new understanding of social responsibility as well.

What then, do pacifist Christians expect from the state?

> *"Everyone must submit himself to the governing authorities, for there is no authority except that which God has established. The authorities that exist have been established by God. Consequently, he who rebels against the authority is rebelling against what God has instituted, and those who do so will bring judgment on themselves. For rulers hold no terror for those who do right, but for those who do wrong. Do you want to be free from fear of the one in authority? Then do what is right and he will commend you. For he is God's servant to do you good. But if you do wrong, be afraid, for he does not bear the sword for nothing. He is God's servant, an agent of wrath to bring punishment on the wrongdoer. Therefore, it is necessary to submit to the authorities, not only because of possible punishment but also because of conscience.*
>
> *"This is also why you pay taxes, for the authorities are God's servants, who give their full time to governing. Give everyone what you owe him: If you owe taxes, pay taxes; if revenue, then revenue; if respect, then respect; if honor, then honor."*
>
> **Romans 13:1-7 (NIV)**

In this classic text for understanding the Christian's relation to the state, the apostle Paul offers both a general summary of the purpose of government and his specific counsel about how followers of Christ should relate to those in political authority. Although many Christians in the past have used these verses in Romans 13 to defend a near-absolute obedience to the state, it is important to take careful note of what Paul actually says here about government, and what he does not say.

Paul begins in verse 1 by admonishing all people, Christians and non-Christians alike, to "be subject to the governing authorities" because ultimately all authority has been established by God. Therefore, anyone who rebels against the authority of governance is rebelling against something that God has instituted (v. 2). This should not be a problem for Christians, however, since the one in authority is "God's servant for your good" (v. 4). The punitive authority of the state, Paul continues, is directed only against those who do wrong. Therefore, Christians do not submit because they fear punishment, but because of their "conscience," that is, their respect for order. Paul then concludes with a series of admonitions: "Give everyone what you owe him: If you owe taxes, pay taxes; if revenue, then revenue; if respect, then respect; if honor, then honor" (v. 7).

> *"Let us not grow weary in doing what is right . . . whenever we have an opportunity, let us work for the good of all, and especially for those of the family of faith."*
> Galatians 6:9-10

What basic themes emerge in this passage?

1. *All authority comes from God.* Authority itself is part of God's character, a necessary means of establishing order. To the degree that the authority of the state contributes to order in a world filled with people who are inclined to do wrong, the state serves a useful function, one that Christians should support. The state is necessary not because it is Christians who are creating disorder, but because of the ongoing sinful nature of the unredeemed.

2. *Christians are to "be subordinate" to the state, giving the state what it is due.* In language similar to the command of Jesus to "give to Caesar that which is Caesar's, and to God that which is God's," Paul tells Christians to "give eneryone what you owe him" (v. 7). But the statement itself does not define the content of what is actually owed. Apart from a call to "be subordinate" and warnings against rebellion, the substance of the Christian obligation to the state is not described here in any detail. It would therefore be misguided to regard this as a command to give carte blanche obedience to everything and anything that the state might demand.

After all, Christians living in the former Soviet Union faced legal restrictions affecting their freedom of worship and their access to Christian literature. Did that mean that those who met secretly or persisted in reading the Bible were violating Paul's teaching? In some conservative Islamic countries, Christianity is forbidden altogether. Does Romans 13 imply that no one should witness to their faith in such a country? No! Surely even Christians tending toward a quite conservative reading of Romans 13 could imagine circumstances in which it would be wrong for Christians to obey an unjust law (for example, a population control measure that made abortions mandatory for all women with two children).

Paul does seem to suggest that Christians should not lead a revolution against the established government. But it would be wrong to argue from this passage that he is trying to eliminate the freedom of the Christian conscience, or that he is turning final authority in matters of faith or religious life completely over to the arm of the state. In Titus, Christians are reminded to "be subject to rulers and authorities, to be obedient, to be ready for every good work" (Titus 3:1), and Peter called on his readers "for the Lord's sake [to] accept the authority of every human institution" (I Peter 2:13).

Yet we know from the history of the early church that Christians in the first three centuries after Christ consistently refused to participate in rituals that recognized the Roman emperors as gods, stubbornly declaring that Christ, not Caesar, was Lord. At the end of the passage in Romans, Christian obedience to the state is clearly premised on the conditional and therefore requires discernment: if taxes, revenue, respect, and honor are due, Paul writes, then grant these things. But only if they are due. In the end, we are to "obey God rather than any human authority" (Acts 5:29).

3. *Pacifist Christians should have rather limited expectations of the state or the political process.* God has established governing authorities because there are forces of disorder in the world. These authorities serve a useful function of restraining evil and protecting the good. Beyond this, however, Paul has little to say about the role of the state, especially compared with the enormous amount of attention he paid to the well-being of the many congregations he helped to establish throughout Asia Minor.

Paul and the other apostles never hesitated to witness openly to their faith when they encountered officials in the

Roman government, but there is no suggestion in the New Testament that the state itself can, or should, embody the principles of love, charity, and nonviolence that are to characterize the witness of the church.

Pacifist Christians might legitimately call the state to live up to its own highest principles—fairness, the rule of law, Just War principles in times of war, and so on. But they do this as informed, concerned citizens, appealing to criteria recognized by all citizens, not as the special pleading of a Christian minority.

4. *The larger context of Romans 13 is a vision of Shalom in which the church, not the state, is the primary focus of God's activity in the world.* In Romans 12, immediately preceding his reflections on governing authorities, Paul instructs the Christians of Rome to a truly radical form of citizenship: "Do not repay anyone evil for evil . . . ," he writes. "No, 'if your enemies are hungry, feed them; if they are thirsty, give them something to drink'" (Romans 12:17, 20). This, however, is an ethic for the Christian and the gathered body of believers. And it is this body, the international community of believers who are committed to living in obedience to Jesus Christ, that is the source of our primary identity and the focus of our deepest allegiance.

Conclusion

Christians in North America have tended to look on faith as something that can improve their lives, not something that might radically reshape their entire worldview. We frequently look on church attendance and faith commitments as something that will make our lives brighter and better—like we regard advertisements for laundry detergent. Only rarely do we consider that the decision to follow Jesus will challenge the very core of our allegiances.

Yet Jesus came to call sinners to repentance. He invites us, like his disciples, to transform not only our hearts but our lives as well; to become members of a new social group that is united around a common commitment to embody Christ's love in daily life.

In this chapter I have suggested that such a commitment should cause us to question the nature of our allegiance to the nation. By refusing to allow the nation or political authorities the last word in matters of ethics, Christians are simply affirming their allegiance to a God whose character has been fully revealed in the life and teachings of Christ.

Allegiance to Christ does not demand that we be anti-American (or anti-Canadian or anti-Belgian for that matter). But it does assume that the confession "Jesus is Lord" has genuine consequences for our lives; it assumes that our primary identity and loyalty are going to be focused first and foremost on Jesus Christ and his church; and it assumes that nothing—not Caesar or the American flag or the principles of democracy or the Western Tradition—transcends the call of Jesus to love our enemies.

In walking in the path of Jesus, trusting fully in God, we bear witness to the power of the resurrection, the power of love over death, and the ultimate triumph of the Lamb.

6.

THE TRANSFORMED POLITICS OF CHRISTIAN CITIZENSHIP

---

*"Build houses and settle down; plant gardens and eat
what they produce. Marry and have sons and daugh-
ters . . . Increase in number there . . . Also, seek the
peace and prosperity of the city to which I have carried
you into exile. Pray to the Lord for it, because if it
prospers, you too will prosper."*

Jeremiah 29:5-7 *(NIV)*

In the summer of 1917 my grandfather, a farm boy from
rural Ohio, was drafted into the United States Army along
with thousands of other young men. Two years earlier, a
German submarine had sunk the British passenger ship
Lusitania with more than 100 U. S. citizens aboard, an event
many Americans considered an act of war. Yet President
Wilson wavered, aware of the enormous costs a commitment
to the European conflict would bring to the nation.

When the United States finally did declare war in April of 1917, most Americans were eager to offer their full support. In a scene repeated around the country, my grandfather's train full of young conscripts left the station to the patriotic tunes of a community band and the boisterous cheers of local townspeople.

Problems began, however, almost as soon as they arrived to begin basic training at Camp Sherman in Chillicothe, Ohio. As a pacifist Christian, my grandfather, along with a handful of others from his community, had decided that he could not in good conscience wear an Army uniform or participate in military training exercises.

Since there were no provisions in the U. S. military code for conscientious objectors, camp officers understandably regarded these actions as an affront to their authority. At first Grandpa was merely assigned to long hours of kitchen duty. But soon other forms of pressure came to bear. At one point several of his friends were called out at night, given shovels, and told to dig their own graves in preparation for their executions at sunrise. Others told of being forced into cold showers and then surrounded by men who scrubbed their skin raw with heavy brooms.

At one point, the commanding officer reported to my grandfather that the other pacifists, including his brother, had relented their position and had agreed to wear the uniform—that he was the only one still holding out. Yet Grandpa persisted in his convictions, and he soon discovered that the officer had lied. Some 60 years later, he could vividly recall the scornful taunts directed at him: coward, slacker, traitor, yellow-bellied parasite.

Grandpa survived Camp Sherman and spent a year in France immediately after the war doing reconstruction work. When he returned home he quickly gained a reputation as a mild-mannered, gentle, and productive member of the community. For much of his life he owned a small neighborhood grocery store, where he was known for his honesty and integrity. In early retirement he became a handyman, doing small repair jobs for local friends, neighbors, and those in need. Throughout his life he contributed generously to worthy causes, paid his bills before they were due, never exceeded the speed limit, and kept his lawn tidier than anyone else's on the block.

He remained a Christian and a pacifist his entire life. Yet when he died at the age of 94, he was remembered not as a coward or a parasite or a traitor to his country, but as an honest, generous, compassionate, and civic-minded person—exactly the kind of model citizen any community would be happy to number among its members.

For many American Christians, the way of peace I have been proposing in this book can sound hopelessly negative—clear in its opposition to war, violence, and patriotic flag-waving, but lacking any constructive plan for meaningful engagement in the world. By placing their loyalty to Christ and his church above that of the nation, pacifist Christians can easily appear to be aloof from their neighbors, disinterested in the civic life of their communities, and automatically critical of every form of national pride.

But aren't Christians also citizens? Don't Christians, even pacifist Christians, participate in economic, political, and cultural realities that extend beyond the church? Shouldn't Christians be working within the structures of society to bring it closer to the Shalom God desires for all people?

In this chapter, I want to respond to these questions with a resounding yes. Despite the fact that pacifist Christians like my grandfather choose *against* violence and war, Christ's way of peace is actually rooted in a profound affirmation, not in negation. Christian pacifism is not "passivism." It does not advocate a retreat from the world, but rather a passionate—and compassionate—commitment to embody the love of Christ in daily life in ways that promote the well-being of the entire community, even if, at times, those efforts run counter to popular opinions. Far from being a threat to the country's welfare, Christian pacifists are catalysts for changed lives and transformed communities, moving both in the direction of God's Shalom.

The Challenge of Linking Faith and Politics

For nearly two millenia, Christians have struggled with the question of how to give appropriate expression to their faith within the economic, political, and cultural institutions of the broader society around them. On the one hand, some Christians have confidently called on fellow believers to mobilize their collective power and to co-opt the machinery of politics and governance in the service of Christ. Whether it be in the medieval mode of crusading armies or the more modern style of direct-mail marketing and no-holds-barred political campaigns, this approach can easily take on the tone of a military campaign, intent on creating an Old Testament-style theocracy in which the church rules over the state, and Christian morality is imposed with the force of law.

At the opposite extreme, a small minority of Christians have withdrawn altogether from the political process. According to their thinking, the way of the cross demonstrated by Jesus is so fundamentally at odds with the logic of politics that the two worlds simply cannot communicate with each other. Christians are redeemed out of the fallen kingdom of the world and called to become citizens of Christ's kingdom alone. The boundaries separating these two kingdoms are as sharp as the line between war and peace, violence and nonviolence, vengeance and compassion.

Clearly, there are at least some elements in both of these options that many Christians would want to affirm. At the same time, however, each position seems locked into an uncreative choice of fight or flight—either storm the gates of governmental power in the name of Christ, in order to impose God's will on the world, or renounce your identity as a citizen and withdraw from politics altogether.

In this chapter I would like to suggest the outlines of a third option—a model of Christian witness in the world that is clear about its primary allegiance to Christ and the gospel of peace yet also ready to fully engage the realities of political and civic life. It seeks to promote Shalom even within the unredeemed structures of the world.

Like the adventure of faith itself, maintaining the balance of this third way is not always easy. It requires a keen attentiveness to God's leading, a persistent commitment to discern the times with wisdom, and a readiness to act both vulnerably and courageously.

Occasionally, as in my grandfather's case, Christian citizens will take positions that go directly against the grain of public opinion, choosing, in their judgment, to "obey God rather than any human authority" (Acts 5:29). Such actions, however, should be understood not as a cowardly retreat from duty, but as a deep and genuine commitment to "seek the welfare of the city" (Jeremiah 29:7). I would like to suggest that in so doing, Christians practice a form of constructive citizenship that contributes significantly to the well-being of their communities and their nations.

The Example of the Early Church

For some clues into the unique nature of Christian citizenship we can start by looking at the example of the early church. In the centuries immediately following Christ's death, Roman officials frequently accused Christians of the same charges leveled against my grandpa: they were parasites, cowards, and traitors who undermined the authority of the Roman government. After all, early Christians did not serve in the army, they refused to offer sacrifices to Caesar, and they preached an ethic of love and humility sharply at odds with the militaristic spirit of Rome. In the eyes of their contemporaries, Christians were a political liability, unworthy of citizenship in the empire.

In the middle of the second century, however, a voice emerged within the Christian community, defending them against these charges and clarifying the nature of Christian citizenship. Sometime around 150 A.D. Justin Martyr, a philosopher by training and a recent convert to Christianity, addressed a lengthy treatise to the emperor Antonius Pius and to the Roman Senate and people. In his *Apology to the Gentiles*, Justin insisted that Christians were not a threat to the political stability of the Empire. To the contrary, they were law-abiding citizens who paid their taxes, respected authority, and were grateful for the orderly life maintained by the Roman emperors. More than that, he went on to argue, in the quality of their personal lives Christians were exemplary citizens:

> *We who formerly delighted in fornication now cleave only to chastity. . . . We who valued above all else the acquisition of wealth and property now direct all that we have to a common fund, which is shared by every needy person. We who hated and killed one another, and who, because of our differing customs,*

> *would not share a fireside with those of another race,*
> *now, after the appearance of Christ, live together with*
> *them. We pray for our enemies, and try to persuade*
> *those who unjustly hate us that, if they lived according*
> *to the same excellent precepts of Christ, they will have*
> *a good hope of receiving the same reward as ourselves*
> *from the God who governs all.*

Justin went on to defend the rapid growth of Christianity as the inevitable consequence of these honorable virtues:

> *Some [converts] were won to Christianity by the*
> *righteousness they observed in the life of their Christian*
> *neighbors. Others were won by the extraordinary*
> *restraint Christian travelers displayed when they were*
> *cheated. Still others were attracted by the honesty of*
> *Christians with whom they transacted business.*

None of these behaviors, Justin insisted, threatened in any way the stability of the Roman empire. Indeed, the distinctive ethical practices promoted by Christianity—mutual aid, compassion for all people, a life of restraint and integrity—were precisely those that every ruler ought to cherish in a people.

History does not record whether Emperor Pius responded to Justin's defense of Christian citizenship or what the Roman Senate thought of his argument. We do know, however, that the basic theme of Justin's argument lived on in the history of the early church.

Sometime toward the end of the third century, we find the following description of how Christians understood their relationship to the state. The passage bears quoting in full because it captures so eloquently the creative way in which members of the early church understood their loyalty to Christ as enhancing the well-being of the society around them:

> *The distinction between Christians and other men is neither in country nor language nor customs. For they do not dwell in cities in some place of their own, nor do they use any strange variety of dialect, nor practice an extraordinary kind of life . . . Yet while living in Greek and barbarian cities—according as each obtained his lot, and following the local customs, both in clothing and food and in the rest of life—they show forth the wonderful and confessedly strange character of the constitution of their own citizenship. They dwell in their own fatherlands, but as if sojourners in them; they have all things as citizens, and suffer all things as strangers . . . To put it shortly, what the soul is in the body the Christians are in the world* (Epistle to Diognetus, V).

As with Justin, the testimony of this anonymous early Christian writer describes Christian citizenship in language that neither denounces the world of politics nor calls on Christians to assert their will through political conquest.

Instead, the author suggests a third way. Christians will inevitably find themselves living in a variety of countries and embracing all manner of languages and local customs. They will "dwell in their own fatherlands" and "have all things as citizens." All of this suggests a wide range of social, cultural, and perhaps even political involvements. But—and this is a crucial caveat—they will do all this as if they were "sojourners" or even "strangers." At home in their local culture, they nonetheless do not ultimately belong to any particular culture, language, or country.

What Justin's *Apology to the Gentiles* and the letter to Diognetus both suggest is a model of citizenship that pulls the Christian into the public square, and at the same time creatively redefines the nature of that civic engagement. Like their neighbors, Christian citizens will attend schools, work in the labor force, contribute to the economy, read newspapers, listen to music, and interact fully with the culture around them. They do this without hesitation, not as a concession to a fallen world, but in the knowledge that God's creation was intended to be good, and that they are called to participate actively in restoring human individuals and the human community to the goodness of their created purpose.

At the same time, however, the motivation, tactics, and goals of Christian citizens will likely be quite different from those around them. Christians will become actively involved in the civic life of their communities, not because they seek political power as an end in itself, because they have experienced the Shalom of God and wish to extend that Shalom wherever they can.

In so doing, the methods they use must be consistent with the character of Jesus Christ. Like Christ, Christian citizens will resist the temptation of short-term expedience. Like Christ, their proposals for healthy relationships will surprise, and perhaps even offend, their audiences. And, like Christ, their tactics will be rooted firmly in love, even if such an approach may sometimes appear naïve and ineffective. After all, for the followers of Jesus the goal of Christian citizenship is not to promote the strength of the nation or to defend a particular ideological political platform. It is rather to extend God's Shalom to every corner of the fallen world.

To speak of Christian citizenship is potentially risky, especially given the long tradition in North American culture that has fused citizenship with patriotism. Christian citizens should never lose sight of the fact that their *pri-*

mary citizenship is in the body of Christ—the church—and that God's will for the world is expressed most fully there, among the gathered body of believers. And yet the church does not exist for itself. Its whole reason for being is to seek the redemption of the world around it.

Thus, like members of the early church, contemporary Christians committed to the way of peace will embrace a way of life shaped by this dynamic tension. As an inevitable consequence of their loyalty to Christ, they will be actively engaged citizens within their communities, testifying to God's gracious love and embodying the gift of Shalom in everything they do.

Getting Specific

What might Christian involvement in political or civic life actually look like? In what ways might Christians share in the activities and practices of non-Christians? What will be distinct about Christian citizenship?

It might be possible for Christian pacifists to participate directly in the political process or to hold political office without compromising their commitment to Christ's way of peace. But, on the surface at least, it seems like a stretch. Apart from the seductive nature of power or the many compromises that are inherent in the political process, most political offices would seem to demand a readiness to support the armed forces and a willingness to use violence in defense of national borders—something a pacifist could not do in good conscience.

Rather than turn our backs on every form of political participation, however, I would like to suggest that Christian pacifists should actively promote a more expansive understanding of political involvement. More than merely governance or a quest for personal power, politics encompasses virtually all of the activities that are related to the public life of the community (*polis*). To the extent that Christian citizens seek to extend the reign of God's Shalom, they will inevitably be involved in political activities, even if they may choose to abstain from some of the formal aspects of political life like office-holding.

Some Christian Responses to War

1. *Pray for peace and for people in government.*

2. *Make every effort to obey the law; however, do not accept military service which involves training in how to kill fellow human beings who are also made in the image of God.*

3. *Join a relief organization to serve unarmed in war zones; provide aid to the victims of war.*

4. *Do not avoid dangerous assignments while doing good; Christians are not cowards.*

5. *Even in honorable professions and businesses, do not exploit the tragedy of war for personal gain.*

6. *Make a living by producing goods and services that sustain life; refuse jobs associated with killing and destruction.*

7. *Be willing to accept the penalties which the state may impose for those who refuse to participate in military action.*

---

8. *Witness to the conviction that Christians who believe that Jesus taught his followers not to kill cannot serve as soldiers, but can willingly serve their country in constructive ways.*

9. *Urge the peaceful resolution of all disputes, while recognizing that leaders of countries are part of this world's system and do not, therefore, rule in full accord with the biblical principle of peace.*

10. *Share the good news of salvation even in time of war.*

Mennonite Brethren statement

The examples of Christian citizenship I offer below suggest the outlines of a more expanded definition of political involvement. They range from the personal to the structural, from the local to the global. They blur the boundaries of public and private. And they encompass programs run by the church, as well as initiatives funded by the state.

It is worth noting that these illustrations of Christian civic engagement are not drawn from a list of unusual initiatives from cities around the country. Nor do they require heroic measures or enormous expenditures of money. Rather, the examples I cite below represent only a small sampling—identified almost at random—of attitudes, individuals, and projects of pacifists Christians that have become part of the social fabric of my rather ordinary, small, midwestern community. In that sense, they reflect the sort of modest local initiatives that are likely occurring in many other places as well.

Significantly, all of the Christian citizens featured in the following pages are pacifists. Most of them wear their pacifism rather lightly, in the sense that they are not aggressively trying to persuade everyone they meet of the absolute truth of their pacifist convictions. But neither is it an accident that their commitment to Christ's way of peace has pulled them into the life of the broader community. In their efforts to testify to God's love, they have found themselves inevitably engaged in politics of one sort or another. In their modest contributions they are offering a glimpse of how God's Shalom is being extended beyond the church into the world around them.

1. The politics of personal ethics: honesty and compassion

Societies function best when their citizens are reasonably assured that promises will be honored, commitments kept, and obligations fulfilled. Good citizens, therefore, regard honesty and integrity as virtues to be practiced in daily life and taught to their children. Because pacifist Christians believe so strongly that their deeds must be aligned with their words, they will be exemplary citizens in the area of personal morality, demonstrating that they are committed to integrity in every aspect of life, whether that be the quality of their marriages, the honesty of their business dealings, or simply the constancy of their characters. If, in rare instances, they disobey the law for the sake of conscience, they will do so publicly and humbly, accepting the legal consequences that may come their way.

Beyond integrity, however, Christian citizens can also be expected to promote the public good by practicing an ethic of compassion. The Christian understanding of compassion tempers the language of rights and justice that dominates much of our current political vocabulary. At the heart of compassion, of course, is the idea of "co-passion" or "shared passion," a willingness to enter genuinely into the thoughts and emotions of another person with a kind and generous spirit.

Compassion is grounded not in pity but in empathy, a readiness to suspend for a moment our own view of the world in order to consider carefully the perspective of another. Compassion calls Christian citizens to honor the dignity of each person and to treat everyone we encounter with the same love that God has extended to us. Christian citizens guided by compassion will inevitably be pulled into relationships with those members of the community who are often living at the margins of society: the poor, the elderly, the young, those without advocates.

What might this mean concretely? One small way that pacifist Christians in my community have expressed compassion is by redefining the boundaries of the nuclear family to make them more porous and inclusive. Bill and Martha, to cite one example, are semi-retired professionals living in my neighborhood. Several years ago they decided to rent their basement apartment to single mothers with the idea that they could serve as friends and mentors to these vulnerable families. Bill and Martha provide a sounding board and the healthy, seasoned perspectives of their own stable relationship for the young women now sharing their home.

In a similar fashion, an older couple in my congregation have become surrogate grandparents for several children in their neighborhood, absorbing some of their reckless energy on behalf of a harried, stressed-out parent, and providing a bright light of structure and unconditional love for children whose lives are otherwise filled with constant uncertainty. Other Christians in my community have become vocal advocates on behalf of foster children, one of the most abused segments of our society, calling attention to the unique challenges these children face and providing a safe haven for several of them in the security of their own homes.

Or consider another example of compassion in action. A college professor by day, Vic loves to spend his off-hours at home, building and tinkering in his small workshop. While his own children were young, Vic became actively involved in the local soap-box derby program and spent hours with his kids building cars and going to races. Several years ago, with his children now largely grown, Vic began to brainstorm with Justin, a young man from his church, about teaming up to build and race a car. Confined to a wheelchair for most of his life, Justin saw the project as a great opportunity, and the two enthusiastically set about their work.

Very quickly, however, they ran into a significant hurdle. Soap-box derby rules required a braking system that would be impossible for someone with Justin's disability to use. Undeterred, Vic designed a well-functioning handbrake. But the rules committee balked, insisting that the established guidelines could not be altered. Still Vic pressed forward, enlisting the support of local businesses and key members of the community.

Thanks to their dogged persistence and the publicity generated by their efforts, the rule was eventually changed. The following year, Justin won a spot in the soap-box derby national championship in Akron, Ohio. Shortly thereafter, Disney executives picked up the heartwarming story and made it into a TV movie called "Miracle in Lane 2."

When Vic began his project with Justin, neither of them ever intended to initiate a reform within the soap-box derby program or to have a television film made of their collaboration. But a simple act of compassion blossomed so that a community rallied around a wonderful cause, the soap-box derby program is now open to children with disabilities, and Disney was inspired to share the story with the whole country.

Personal integrity and compassion, of course, are virtues that are not exclusive to pacifist Christians, and they may seem like relatively insignificant political gestures. But for Christians committed to Christ's way of peace, these attitudes and actions are not optional. They are the heart of Christian faith. And the public commitment of Christians to demonstrate honesty and compassion in all their relationships provides a sure foundation on which to build thriving neighborhoods and communities. In this sense, Christian pacifists are model citizens.

2. The politics of community transformation

Sociologists from Alexis de Tocqueville to Robert Bellah have long argued that the health of a democratic society ultimately rests on a network of voluntary groups and informal associations that give communities their distinctive textures and identities. Little League baseball teams, parent-teacher organizations, reading groups, babysitting coops, farmers' markets, bowling leagues, investment clubs, and service groups—all of these grassroots institutions bring together people of various ethnic, social, economic, and religious backgrounds into relationships that build trust and a healthy sense of community. Voluntary associations cannot replace government, but they do help to train people in the skills of democracy. They also create a context beyond the partisanship of party politics to celebrate the common good.

To be sure, not only Christians participate in such groups. But in addition to joining with others in community associations, Christians should be expected to push beyond established patterns to help create new forms of social interaction that had not previously existed. Consider once more several local examples in which pacifist Christians have taken the lead in developing grassroots organizations that have contributed significantly to the well-being of the entire community.

La Casa

Over the past two or three decades, sustained economic growth has attracted a large number of new residents to our area, a region whose economy is heavily dependent on wage labor. Initially, many of these newcomers, especially the immigrants from Mexico, found themselves in a precarious economic and social position, uprooted from the web of connections in their home communities and uncertain about their future here.

In 1974, several local Christians began a small ministry called LaCasa (The Home) that was intended to help new residents in the community, especially Spanish-speaking newcomers, find low-income housing. Over the years, the program has grown enormously, steadily adapting in response to new needs as circumstances and opportunities changed.

In 2001, LaCasa provided direct assistance to nearly 500 families. In addition to maintaining over 100 low-income rental units, the organization has developed an innovative home savings and loan program combined with a "financial fitness" training program that recently honored some 92 graduates. LaCasa now has a food pantry and referral advocacy program for crisis needs, a translation service designed especially to assist immigrants in getting their documents in order, and a citizenship training initiative that provides newcomers to the area with a basic grounding in English, along with an orientation to local legal and cultural nuances. Seeking to promote long-term wholistic changes within the community, LaCasa has been a pioneer in the concept of neighborhood revitalization, targeting resources and energy to specific neighborhoods, rather than scattering their efforts haphazardly throughout the community.

Over the past decade, LaCasa has begun to gain widespread attention beyond our community. Recently its long-term director accepted an invitation from a major U. S. city to establish a similar program based on this local model.

Thus, in a small but persistent way, LaCasa has been a catalyst to promote Shalom, making our community more hospitable to newcomers and improving the quality of life for all residents, new and old alike.

Bridgework Theater

As a recent graduate from college, Don's passion for writing was matched only by his love of drama. When he started Bridgework Theater in 1979, he admits that his main goal was simply to find a way to get paid for doing what he loved to do. If he could use theater to express his Christian convictions, so much the better. The original plan was to get social service agencies to fund educational dramas on topics relevant to their concerns. One of the first dramas he wrote, a play addressing the highly sensitive problem of the sexual abuse of children, met with enormous success in elementary schools throughout the region, drawing high praise from teachers, administrators, and social service professionals.

Since that modest beginning, Bridgework Theater has given more than 6,400 performances to nearly 2,000,000 children. Based on systematic surveys of elementary school students and teachers, Don has frequently shifted the focus of his plays to respond to the changing issues of the day. Currently, his dramas revolve around themes of conflict resolution, anger management, and the relational challenges of empathy and bullying.

Bridgework Theater is not an explicitly Christian drama company. Its three troupes of actors cannot pretend to resolve the profound problems of abuse and violence that children face each day. But the plays they perform are deeply rooted in Don's commitment to Christ's way of peace, and the stories that unfold on stage offer audiences a glimpse of God's hope for healthy human relationships built on trust and intimacy.

Like LaCasa, Bridgework Theater is an expression of political engagement, one that is pointing a generation of children toward emotional maturity and helping to strengthen the civic fabric of the broader community.

Friends of the Pumpkinvine Nature Trail, Inc.

For nearly all of his life John has been an avid biker. In addition to the exercise, he enjoys the companionship of a group excursion, and he loves the opportunity biking provides to see the local landscape from a new perspective. But biking for John is also an expression of Christian citizenship. In a culture that has made the automobile into something of a god—to which we sacrifice enormous sums of money in highway construction, fossil fuels, accident insurance, and litigation—riding a bicycle is a healthy expression of counter-cultural stewardship.

When a nationwide movement began in the 1980s to

convert abandoned railroad lines to bike paths, the Rails to Trails initiative, John became an enthusiastic supporter of the idea. His initial efforts, however, met with strong resistance from landowners adjacent to the local railroad line. So John stepped back and began to organize from the grassroots. He formed a not-for-profit organization, The Friends of the Pumpkinvine Nature Trail, Inc., conducted surveys, published newsletters, wrote editorials, explored funding possibilities, and pursued a crash course in property rights law.

Along the way, John's efforts encouraged local city officials to take interest in the idea of a linear park within the city limits where support for bike paths was much stronger. In short order, the mayor's office and city park department secured federal money to construct a network of bike trials linking virtually every park and neighborhood in the community.

Meanwhile, progress on John's project continued to face strong opposition. So far, only a few miles of his dream have been completed, and the debate has stretched the limits of civility on both sides of the controversy. But his efforts have brought dozens of people into important conversations about the nature of the public good. His work spurred the city into action on a linear park system that is now heavily used. And John has helped to plant the tiny seed of an idea in the minds of many people that our national commitment to the automobile should be balanced with modest investments in other forms of transportation.

Although each of these initiatives intersected in some significant way with politics in the traditional sense, none of the people involved in these activities would describe themselves as a politician. In each instance, the inspiration for their actions emerged out of a worldview rooted in their commitment to Christ's way of peace. Starting from that foundation they found themselves being pulled into the life of the broader community. As with most pacifists, their commitment to peace did not stop at saying "no" to violence and war. To the contrary. Christ calls his followers to pursue the well-being of the broader communities, to say "yes" to God's Shalom and "the welfare of the city."

3. The politics of "double vision"

In his insightful book on Christian reconciliation titled *Exclusion and Embrace*, the Croatian theologian Miroslav Volf calls on Christians to cultivate a perspective that he calls "double vision."[1] Double vision is the ability to view the world simultaneously in its particularity—shaped, as it is, by our local cultural biases and provincial understandings—and from a global perspective, or "through the eyes of God." For Christian citizens, double vision suggests a capacity both to participate fully within the life of our communities or countries, while also recognizing that we are part of a larger global community.

Double vision does not imply that we should turn in our passports and somehow become citizens of the world. We are always going to be rooted in particular political contexts and shaped by specific languages and the contours of our local cultures. But the gift of double vision does mean that we can define Christian citizenship in such a way that our local identities and loyalties are deepened and enriched by a broader awareness of those beyond our borders.

Double vision helps us to guard against the narrowness of our caricatures and prejudices. It pushes us beyond the temptation to interpret all of life through the near-sighted perspectives of local or national identity. Because

Christians recognize that *all* humans—not just those in our own community or nation, have been made in the image of God, and because Christians serve a Christ who is Lord of *all* peoples, they will be quick to recognize the shared bonds of humanity that unite us across national and cultural boundaries. This kind of Christian double vision can take dozens of different forms. I will highlight several modest examples from my community.

MEDA (Mennonite Economic Development Associates)
Kevin is a successful businessman whose family operates a local flea market and livestock auction. Over the years, the family has steadily expanded the scope of their business so that it now attracts some 30,000 people to the area every weekend and has come to have a significant economic impact on the entire region.

By all accounts, Kevin is a solid businessman, highly regarded by his peers. Yet as a Christian committed to the way of peace, he has not been content to simply maximize his profits locally. For nearly two decades, Kevin has been an active member of MEDA (Mennonite Economic Development Associates), an international organization committed to serving the poor by providing credit, business and marketing training, and other technical assistance to entrepreneurs in the United States and abroad.

Since its beginnings in 1953, MEDA has grown beyond the wildest dreams of its founders. In 2001, MEDA numbered some 3,000 members who together have invested in nearly 3,800 micro-enterprise projects in nine countries and offer on-going business counseling services in dozens of additional countries. Each year these initiatives create or sustain some 10,000 jobs around the world.

"My initial attraction to MEDA," Kevin admits, "was

somewhat selfish. I was looking for a place to network with other people who were serious about connecting their faith with the world of business. I was looking for contacts." But as his involvement with MEDA deepened, Kevin began to realize that the benefits of his involvement went far beyond mere networking. In his travels to Haiti, Cuba, Paraguay, and Ethiopia, for example, he has developed friendships with people from vastly different cultures and has discovered along the way that they are facing many of the same questions and challenges in their businesses as he does. "I've also come to realize that God is alive and at work on the other side of the world, just as much as He is present here in North America. We serve a big God, a God who cares about all of us."

A long-time member of MEDA's national board of directors, Kevin is deeply committed to the group's philosophy of mutual assistance: "MEDA is not about giving people handouts and creating relationships of dependency. Instead, we are committed to helping each other learn how to become successful in our businesses in ways that treat people fairly and honor God."

By bringing dozens of businesspeople like Kevin into partnerships with poor people around the world, MEDA offers a reminder that there are ways of doing business based on principles deeper than the economic calculation of the bottom line. MEDA provides evidence of relationships on an international scale that fly in the face of the crass commercialism and the relentless quest for profits driving much of the global economy today.

Christian Peacemaker Teams
Janet graduated from college in 1982 with a degree in sociology. After spending several years as a volunteer in

Louisiana helping a Hispanic/Native American community gather oral traditions and compile family histories, she returned to school and completed a masters degree in anthropology. Janet always had a keen desire to put her faith into action, especially her commitment to peace. But it was not clear to her just what form that commitment should take. While working in a college library in my community, Janet became aware of an organization called Christian Peacemaker Teams (CPT).

CPT was founded in 1986 in the conviction that pacifist Christians should be willing to take risks on behalf of those who are suffering from injustice, domination, and the violence of war. At the invitation of local peacemakers, CPT sends teams of North American volunteers into situations of conflict around the world. Trained in peacemaking skills, CPT members bear witness to the injustice and violence present in these settings and seek nonviolent resolutions to the conflicts. On the basis of their first-hand experience, CPT members keep interested citizens and policymakers informed about the nature of the conflict and try to help North American Christians identify more actively with the injustice and suffering of others.

At first, Janet served in CPT's "reserve corps," spending three to six weeks in places like Port-au-Prince, Haiti, or Chiapas, Mexico, and the West Bank city of Hebron. Each time upon her return, Janet reported on what she had seen and learned to church groups, civic organizations, and college students. After some three years as a reservist, Janet quit her job in the library and became a full-time member of CPT, committing herself to a mission of peacemaking even at the risk of her own physical safety. Recently, she returned to Hebron where she was part of a team documenting the destruction of Palestinian homes, listening to voices of anger and hope, and standing alongside victims of violence. She and her fellow workers write regular reports about the personal pain they are witnessing on the ground in this protracted and bitter conflict. Unlike MEDA, CPT is a relatively small organization. Sometimes, its readiness to move quickly into complex situations of violence can sound like a distant echo of Don Quixote. Yet in their determination to bear witness to the pain of the world and to seek creative alternatives to violence, Janet and her CPT colleagues are acting out a vision of Christian citizenship that is faithful to their understanding of a God who longs for all people to live in peace.

Seniors for Peace

In 1986, as a 72-year-old, Atlee had the sparkle in his eye and the bounce in his step of a much younger person. For more than 50 years, Atlee had been active in a host of peacemaking efforts. Following World War II, he volunteered as a relief and reconstruction worker in Europe. In the decades that followed, he frequently interrupted his career as a professor of psychology for prolonged periods of service in locations around the world. From 1966 to 1974, at the height of the Vietnam War, he served as the head of an inter-religious relief organization in that ravaged country. In the early 1980s he and his wife helped to establish an educational exchange program with a teaching college in China. In the late 1980s he assisted in reconciliation efforts in Ireland—to list only a few of his involvements.

By the summer of 1986, Atlee would have had good reason to ease into a quiet retirement and let other, presumably younger, people pick up the tasks at hand. But driven by a deep sense of compassion for the suffering of others, Atlee developed a vision for mobilizing the energies of retirees in the community for the cause of peace. So, along with his wife and four friends, Atlee established Seniors for Peace.

In many regards, Seniors for Peace looks a lot like other grassroots organizations dedicated to speak out on behalf of peace and justice. Over the years, members have addressed such issues as nuclear proliferation, land mines, human rights violations, the death penalty, and war toys. In addition to organizing forums for education and discussion, Seniors for Peace members have worked with prisoners in local jails, witnessed against the death penalty, hosted prayer vigils, and established a Peace Center at a local congregation. They have written countless letters of protest and support to political and religious leaders, to newspaper editors, to the oppressed, "and to those designated as enemies."

"In everything I have done," says Atlee, "my goal has been to bring together God's unrationed grace and God's call to reconciling ministry." For Atlee, participation in Seniors for Peace "provides motivation and meaning to my soul and confirms that peacemaking is my vocation."[2]

Kevin, Janet, and Atlee all serve the cause of Christian citizenship by practicing the gift of double vision. From a global vantage point, their actions are extremely modest in scope. Nevertheless, in their efforts to bridge the limited perspectives of the local community with the broader realities of the world, they remind us that Christ's message of reconciliation is indeed for all people.

4. The politics of "selective disengagement"
The examples I have given thus far have suggested several creative ways of engaging in the political life of the community while testifying to the gospel of peace, which

is at the heart of Christian faith. Still other pacifist individuals and groups in my community have felt compelled by their Christian conscience to bear witness to God's Shalom by selectively withdrawing from specific kinds of social and political involvement.

In each instance, the individuals making these decisions consider themselves U.S. citizens and openly express their gratitude for the many positive aspects of North American life. But at the same time, they have tried to find ways of maintaining a clear boundary between the church, where their primary allegiance lies, and the state, which they respect but whose authority must be ultimately subject to the claims of Christ.

Choosing not to litigate

When Ralph's long-time business partner and friend first started coming into work late, he tried not to let it irritate him. The relationship had not always been smooth, but Ralph and his partner had managed to forge a highly successful business that was just now moving into a new level of profitability. Each of them brought a different set of abilities to the business. Ralph was a risk-taking entrepreneur, a genius at recognizing how to adapt existing technologies to new uses. His partner was the sober-minded accountant who kept the cash flow intact and the books balanced.

During the early years of the business, when profits were slim to nonexistent, the two spent hours together consulting and adapting their strategies in response to the volatility of the market. Now that the business had greatly expanded, Ralph and his partner met far less frequently. And in recent months, Ralph had noticed a growing edginess in his partner's demeanor. When he finally decided to confront his partner about the changed quality of their relationship, his friend exploded in anger. That tense meeting led to a series of other angry confrontations.

Only several months later did the source of his partner's new attitude become clear. A closer look at the books revealed that Ralph's partner had been steadily siphoning off company profits into private bank accounts. Even worse, through a series of dubious maneuvers, the partner had effectively gained operational control over the company.

A business consultant called it a clear case of criminal fraud. "A trial will be messy," the consultant noted, "but the legal facts are absolutely clear. There's no judge in the country who wouldn't rule in your favor."

For most of Ralph's associates, the next steps were patently obvious: hire an attorney, take the partner to court, and demand that justice be served. For Ralph, however, the matter was not so clear. As a deeply committed Christian, he took seriously Christ's words to his disciples that disputes, especially among believers, were not to be settled in secular courts.

After praying about the matter for several weeks and discussing it with members of his church, Ralph decided to pursue a different strategy. He and two other members of his congregation asked for a meeting with his partner and the pastor of his partner's church. At the meeting, the three laid out the facts as they were able to reconstruct them. "It is clear that Ralph has been treated unfairly," the group stated, "but we have decided that we will not resolve this in a court of law. We come to you as Christian brothers in the church, asking that you make this a matter of conscience and a question of discipline within your own congregation."

The process that followed that initial meeting was sometimes confused and even tortuous. But eventually, with the help of a mediator and some courageous pastoral intervention, Ralph and his partner were able to resolve their differences. The financial settlement Ralph agreed to may have been less generous than a court would have awarded, but he does not regret his decision.

> *Instead of an "eye for an eye," Jesus said, "Love your enemies and pray for those who persecute you."*
> Matthew 5:38,44

Clearly, the vulnerable process of church discipline in accordance with the pattern established in Matthew 18, a process backed by the discernment of the community rather than the coercive power of the courts, offered no guarantee of success. But it was a path consistent with Ralph's understanding of the gospel and the centrality of peace to the life of the Christian. By disengaging himself from the litigious culture of modern society, Ralph testifies both to his freedom from the bondage of wealth and the power of the Christian community to resolve conflicts in a manner consistent with Christ's teachings.

Abstaining from the national anthem

In the months following the attacks of September 11, one of the many visible changes in the national landscape was the sudden presence of the American flag. Overnight, it seemed, the flag began to appear not just outside public buildings, but on front lawns, in picture windows, hanging from porch railings, and attached to car antennas. The impulse to express national solidarity through the flag was so powerful that some residents in my community even wrote curt letters to the local newspapers complaining about neighbors who were slow to hoist the colors.

For one local Christian school, the flood of flags and outpouring of patriotic sentiment poised a challenging dilemma. Throughout its 50-year history, Bethany Christian Schools had never had a flag in its gymnasium, nor did it have a tradition of singing the national anthem prior to athletic events. The school was not trying to be anti-American. Instead, it was simply giving concrete expression to a conviction that God's people are defined by loyalties that transcend national allegiances and patriotic symbols.

In the aftermath of September 11, however, visiting basketball teams and their fans began to express public disapproval. How could it be that a school would not rally behind the nation in a time of national crisis? Shouldn't all Americans be required to salute the flag or sing the national anthem? As the criticisms mounted, school officials met with teachers, parents, and the board to discuss an appropriate response.

Community sentiment was clear; the temptation to relent to public pressure was powerful. Yet, in the end, Bethany Christian Schools decided, respectfully, that current events did not change the principles behind the original decision. In a statement printed in the basketball program guide, school officials explained their position in the following words:

> Bethany Christian Schools chooses not to play the national anthem at athletic events based on our conviction that allegiance to Jesus Christ transcends allegiance to any nation. At the same time, we deeply appreciate the many good things about our nation and take seriously our responsibility to pray for our lead-

ers and contribute to the well-being of our communities. We hope that schools playing at Bethany can respect this conviction in the same way we respect the national anthem being sung or played in other schools.

The decision may well prove costly to the school, both in terms of community goodwill and financial support. But the school will undoubtedly continue to produce teachers and doctors and business persons who will emerge as leaders in the community. And these future leaders will serve the community even better, knowing there are times when the commitments of Christian conscience take precedence over the pressures of public opinion.

A Life of Economic Simplicity

Tim and Susan were both on upwardly mobile tracks to professional success. Before he was 25, Tim, a computer software designer in a major corporation, was already earning more money than he had ever thought possible. Susan was an office manager at a large law firm. Though the hours were long and the work demanding, she too was making enough money to afford all of the amenities of the "good life." By virtually any standard, Tim and Susan were well on their way to achieving the American Dream.

And yet, despite their high-paying jobs, expensive vacations, and designer clothes, both of them sensed that something significant was missing. "We slowly came to realize," said Tim, "that our lives revolved around our credit cards, our stock portfolios, and the things we were steadily accumulating. And we still weren't happy! There was no focus or meaning to what we were doing."

As a result of a friendship with someone from work, Tim and Susan began attending a local church. Over time, they reached a decision to become Christians and to embrace the gospel of peace. That decision was to have a radical impact on their lives—one that surprised even them. "It slowly became clear to us," reflected Susan, "that peacemaking and economics are closely related. The United States currently consumes a hugely disproportionate amount of the world's resources. And many of our recent wars have been fought over our control of limited resources and our desire to maintain our current standard of living."

In response to that awareness, Tim and Susan have decided, along with many other Christian pacifists, to "selectively disengage" themselves from the economic assumptions of our culture. Both have found new jobs more aligned with their new priorities of time and resources. Through donations to charities, they are now living at the poverty line. And they are finding new meaning in life by challenging, at least symbolically, assumptions of the economic world around them—by consciously resisting the allure of fashion and style, by recycling as much waste as possible, and by walking "more lightly" on the world.

Withholding war taxes

Some Christian pacifists have been deeply troubled about the double standard they see in the fact that a significant portion of their federal income tax, perhaps as much as 50%, goes directly to support a military and defense budget that they find morally objectionable. How, they ask themselves, can we "pray for peace while paying for war"? For nearly 20 years, Michael and Anna have tried to resolve this inner struggle of conscience by withholding that portion of their federal income tax that goes to the military.

This is not an action that Michael and Anna hide from the government. Each year they send a letter along with their tax return, informing the IRS exactly what they are doing and giving a rationale for their actions. They are not seeking to undermine the authority of the state, nor are they challenging the basic right of a government to collect taxes. Like many other tax resisters, Michael and Anna pay state and local taxes. They gladly support the local public education system, road maintenance, and government-funded social services. They resist only the portion of their federal income tax that is designated for the military.

The point of their action is explicitly not for their personal material gain. In fact, each spring they write a check for the amount of the tax dollars they have withheld from the IRS to support the work of a charitable, not-for-profit organization.

Those who disagree with Michael's and Anna's actions frequently cite the passage from Matthew 22: "Give therefore to the emperor the things that are the emperor's, and to God the things that are God's" (v. 21b). But this passage, they insist, hardly resolves the matter, since Jesus here is simply admonishing his listeners to do the hard work of discernment. In other words, Christians are to sort carefully through exactly what belongs to the emperor and what belongs to God, and then act accordingly. Michael and Anna believe that the military portion of their income tax belongs to God.

The couple has strongly supported the Peace Tax Fund Bill, which has come before Congress every year since 1972 and would permit taxpayers to designate the military portion of their taxes to peaceful purposes. If the bill were passed, Michael and Anna would gladly pay the full portion of their federal taxes. Until that time, however, they will continue this gesture of conscientious objection to military spending and live with the economic and legal consequences that come their way.

Refusing to litigate, choosing a life of simplicity, abstaining from the national anthem, or withholding war taxes does not exhaust the ways in which Christians committed to the gospel of peace have "selectively disengaged" themselves from the assumptions of the culture around them. Some other Christians I know, for example, have consciously decided *not* to dial 911, nor to solicit the coercive power of the police if they faced a threat to their property or personal security. Some have opted out of traditional health insurance policies or the Social Security program, preferring to rely on the mutual assistance of the church in times of financial need.

And even though many individuals in these groups would vote in local or state elections, some have even chosen not to participate in national elections, especially not presidential campaigns. "One of the responsibilities of the president is to serve as commander in chief of the Armed Forces," one member stated. "If I could not in good conscience serve in that position, how can I then cast my vote of support for someone else to serve in my place?"

> *"I am sending you out like sheep into the midst of wolves; so be wise as serpents and innocent as doves."*
>
> Matthew 10:16

Those in the mainstream of American Christianity will likely find it easy to dismiss these voices of selective disengagement as eccentric, naïve, inconsistent, or even socially irresponsible. And yet each of these choices reflects a conscientious effort on the part of pacifist Christians to move from an abstract view of faith to a more concrete expression of God's call, even if it challenges standard assumptions about politics and economics. In their more radical approach to Christian discipleship, these individuals provide additional threads of witness within the colorful fabric of the gospel of peace.

5. The politics of presence, patience, and persistence

Every community has at least one saint. Often it is someone who quietly and steadily moves into circumstances of need and, often beneath the radar of public fanfare, helps hurting people find solutions to their problems. In my community, the closest person to a saint that I know (though, like all saints, she would be aghast to be identified as such) is Mary Ellen. For nearly four decades, Mary Ellen has been a tireless advocate for people at the very edges of our community. Though she draws no salary, she has had a significant impact on the lives of dozens of individuals and has quietly elevated the quality of life for the entire community.

"I have never been able to shake the reality of growing up in a position of privilege," Mary Ellen reflected. "Why was I born into a loving home with opportunities for education and travel, and with no financial worries? If you've been given these privileges and think about justice, then you somehow find yourself compelled to extend a hand to others."

Trained as a nurse, Mary Ellen set aside her aspirations to become a medical doctor in order to raise a family of five children. As a young mother, she became aware of studies showing the crucial importance of cognitive stimulation in early childhood for the emotional development of healthy adults. So she started a preschool in her local congregation, intended for infants of single mothers, who also benefited from the positive social interaction and modeling that the school provided.

From there, Mary Ellen moved into healthcare advocacy, especially for children and low-income families. Along with others, she was instrumental in establishing a clinic in one of the community's poorest neighborhoods. Concerned about the growing number of elderly who could not afford nursing care, Mary Ellen promoted home healthcare for the elderly and helped initiate a local Meals on Wheels program to ensure that those most in need would have at least one personal contact and a nourishing meal each day.

In the past decade, Mary Ellen has put most of her energies into the life of a new congregation, one committed to building sustained relationships between rich and poor. There she has pursued a ministry of "availability." "Every day is different," she mused. "I simply try to be available for whatever happens to come up." Usually that includes accompanying people to appointments—the doctor's office, the lawyer, a court date, a social service agency—where she serves as an advocate and guide through the labyrinthine maze of bureaucratic procedures that often intimidate those she is serving. Along the way she offers a listening ear, the benefit of a broad perspective, and the gift of companionship and respect for every person she engages.

What Mary Ellen brings to her Christian citizenship are qualities that ultimately transcend any particular area of expertise or specific act of kindness. At the heart of her politics are the Christian gifts of presence, patience, and persistence.

All Christian-inspired politics begin with *presence,* with a willingness to stand in those places of risk and vulnerability that allow God's Spirit to break through in surprising and transforming ways. Traditional politics, of course, assume that these spaces will be in the glare of the public spotlight. Yet the gift of presence offered by the Christian citizen will often happen away from center stage, in the middle of the pain and brokenness of real people, offering no promise of future power or glory. "Let us give our hand to all those around the world who suffer, who cry out and are fearful," writes Jean Vanier in the *Catholic Worker.* "Let us remember that the smallest gesture of beauty and tenderness done with humility and confidence will . . . break the chain of violence."

The gift of *patience* is also one not frequently honored in standard political circles. Public attention spans are fleeting, the media moves like a hummingbird from topic to topic, and lobbying groups demand quick responses to their entreaties. Christians, having a more humble perspective on their ability to control the future, can appreciate the fact that social and political change frequently takes time. It's not that Mary Ellen is resigned to the status quo. But she recognizes that the habits and patterns of behavior of the people with whom she works are not generally going to be undone overnight. Nor is any single issue that she has engaged—child advocacy, healthcare, or assistance to the elderly—going to be fixed with the introduction of a single program or initiative. "If you expect to see the final results of your work," journalist I. F. Stone has written, "you simply have not asked a big enough question."

Finally, Christian citizens offer their communities the gift of *persistence.* Every day, Mary Ellen encounters disappointments and frustrations that would tempt many of us to throw up our hands in despair. The problems—deep-seated addictions, cycles of violence, dysfunctional relationships—are so complex, so immense, so overwhelming. And yet for all of her life, Mary Ellen has stubbornly refused to give up. Now in her 70s, she brings the same quiet, cheerful determination to her ministry that she did 50 years ago. "All I am doing," she says, "is trying to see that which is of God in everybody—to see people with the dignity that God has given to each person. Sometimes I despair, but people do change."

Because Christians know that history is unfolding in God's time, not ours, we can press on, even if the outcome seems uncertain. In the words of Christian activist Jim Wallis: "It is not the achievement of success, but rather the giving of ourselves in faith that leads to life."

Summary

In previous chapters I have suggested that the decision to follow Christ involves more than a cosmetic change. Becoming a Christian implies an entirely new perspective on reality itself, a new way of seeing God's presence in the world that allows us to trust completely in Him, in the knowledge that God's love is stronger than our fears.

Such an approach to life may appear to be hopelessly unrealistic, irresponsible, or out-of-touch with the real world. A commitment to nonviolence may sound noble enough, but in reality it seems to allow evil to flourish, to turn its back on the suffering of innocents, and to dismiss the virtues of citizenship that are the underpinnings of democracy and law.

In this chapter, I have tried to put some of those fears to rest. Pacifist Christians, I suggest, are not anarchists seeking to undermine the authority of government. They are instead courageous citizens, driven by a vision of the "good society" that compels them to act in ways that seek the welfare of the entire community. They are not perfect—either in their personal lives nor in their public actions—and critics will have no difficulty in discovering inconsistencies in their thoughts and deeds.

But Christian citizens are committed to putting their ideals into action in ways that reflect the same generous love and compassion they have received from God. Confessing their faults in all humility, they nonetheless press on not only to proclaim the good news of the gospel, but to embody it in their daily lives and to invite others to participate in that good news. In so doing, God's Shalom extends beyond the church to the community as well.

---

[1] Miroslav Volf, *Exclusion and Embrace: A Theological Exploration of Identity, Otherness and Reconciliation* (Nashville: Abingdon Press, 1996), 212-220.

[2] Atlee Beechy, *Seeking Peace: My Journey* (Goshen, IN: Pinchpenny Press, 2001), 177.

CONCLUSION

". . . Things fall apart; the center cannot hold;
Mere anarchy is loosed upon the world,
The blood-dimmed tide is loosed, and everywhere
The ceremony of innocence is drowned;
The best lack all conviction, while the worst
Are full of passionate intensity."
William Butler Yeats, *The Second Coming* (1922)

"The best lack all conviction, while the worst are full of passionate intensity." As the twentieth century came to a close, these lines from the Irish poet William Butler Yeats captured with apt precision the cultural mood of our time.

By any reckoning, the century just past was filled with enough "passionate intensity" to make it one of the bloodiest epochs in all of human history. The century's violence began early in 1898 with an alleged act of terrorism, the explosion of the battleship *Maine* as it sat in the harbor of Havana, killing nearly 300 people aboard, and the ensuing Spanish-American War.

Scarcely a decade later, World War I decisively shattered the pious illusion that European nations had become too civilized for war. Over a four-year period at least nine million young men died in a war that witnessed the introduction of mobile tanks, improved machine guns, concertina wire, land mines, bombs dropped from airplanes, and chemical warfare. By mid-century the scale of violence and destruction of this "war to end all wars" had been matched, and then surpassed, by a second world war that claimed the lives of at least 50 million more victims and made household words of "Pearl Harbor," the "Holocaust," and "Hiroshima."

In the aftermath of World War II, a new kind of despot emerged—Joseph Stalin, Mao Tse Tung and Pol Pot were its best exemplars—in which the quest for totalitarian control came at the expense of perhaps another 75-80 million lives, most of them "disappeared" into mass, anonymous graves.

During the second half of the century, a nuclear arms race brought the superpowers to the brink of "mutually assured destruction." Grinding wars in Vietnam, Afghanistan, and the Middle East revealed that superpowers could not impose their military will on recalcitrant populations. Ethnic cleansings in Rwanda, the Balkans, and Indonesia dominated headlines throughout the 1990s. And on September 11, 2001—almost before the century had really begun—the U.S. declared "the first war of the twenty-first century" against the elusive target of international terrorism.

Looking back now from the perspective of a century of history, the poet's worried gaze on the future seemed to be well founded. The twentieth century has indeed been awash in a "blood-dimmed tide." Anarchy has repeatedly been "loosed upon the world." Today only the hopelessly naïve could speak of a "ceremony of innocence."

At the same time, Yeats' poem reveals still another, equally troubling insight about the nature of modern culture. Not only is it true that "the worst are full of passionate intensity," but, as he noted with prescience, "the best lack all conviction."

CONCLUSION

We live, it seems, in the grip of a profound paradox. Even as the "passionate intensity" of ideologues, dictators, fundamentalists, and terrorists has led to the violent death of millions of people, the twentieth century also witnessed a spiritual and intellectual crisis of conviction that has cast doubt on the very moral frameworks that should have been challenging the violence of our age.

What started as a well-intended critique of power in the Enlightenment tradition of systematic doubt, slowly took on a life of its own in the last half of the twentieth century in the form of postmodernism. Captivated by the seductive logic of deconstructionism, thoughtful people have found it increasingly difficult to express *any* conviction about truth. For postmodernists, claims regarding truth are merely Nietzschean expressions of power, sophisticated efforts to conceal the will to dominate others. Thus, thinking it to be a generosity of spirit, some of the "very best" among us "lack all conviction" and have become paralyzed into passivity, incapable of making moral judgments or discerning the difference between good and evil.

"You shall not kill."
Exodus 20:13 *(RSV)*

For most modern people, the options sketched by Yeats seem equally foreboding—either the callous and violent intensity of passionate belief or the banal etiquette of an accommodating relativism; either the white-knuckled fundamentalism of the warrior or the passive disengagement from all moral judgments of the sophisticated scholar.

In this book I have tried to suggest that there is a third option. In contrast to most postmodern thinkers, I have described a universe created by God who actively invites human beings into relationships of trust and intimacy. It is a universe structured ultimately not by coercion and fear, but by the power of love. For this reason, those who are suspicious of all claims about truth need not be afraid that this assertion is one more power-move. Indeed, the very essence of the good news of the Christian gospel is that our God is a noncoercive God who invites rather than compels. The Jesus we claim as Lord came to us in the form of a servant, taught an ethic of vulnerability and compassion, and allowed himself to be killed rather than to take up the sword and defend the truth with violence.

Here in the space created by Christ's way of peace and reconciliation we find a place to stand that succumbs neither to the violence of "passionate intensity" nor the vapid relativism of the "absence of convictions."

The good news of the gospel is that God loved us even though we were not worthy of that love, "while we were still enemies of God," and, in Christ, offered the free gift of forgiveness and reconciliation. This part is familiar. But we don't fully claim the gospel as good news unless we recognize that those who have received God's gracious, undeserved gift of love will inevitably seek to express that same love to others, including (indeed, especially) our enemies.

If this is the Christ that we claim as our Savior—a nonviolent, compassionate, gracious Lord—then we can witness to that truth in both confidence and humility. Our tone will be invitational, but not combative; testimonial, but not argumentative; joyful, but not defensive; inclusive, but not relativistic.

1. In God We Trust: Made in the image of God, we are nonetheless endowed with the freedom to reject that part of our nature and to pursue a way of life dedicated to defending the self by relying on our own energy and strength. A Christian worldview recognizes this deep impulse in human beings toward self-reliance, as well as the fear that is generated when humans acknowledge their own finitude and mortality. Christian faith begins with a clear recognition of our vulnerability and dependence. Faith is a response to God's invitation to trust in Him alone and to acknowledge that every moment of our lives is shaped by His mercy and sustaining love.

2. *Jesus is Lord:* In Jesus Christ, the world finds the fullest expression of God's character. Here, too, we find the fullest expression of Shalom, a model of how human beings are to live in harmony with God, with each other, and with the natural world. Since Jesus is God Incarnate, he comes to us as Lord of the entire world, not just as Lord over myself, my family, my denomination, or my nation. Moreover, Jesus comes to us as Lord over the principalities and powers of evil and hatred and destruction and, indeed, death itself. Thus, to proclaim Jesus as Lord is to participate in a reality that transcends the bonds of society and politics, and that frees us from the human bondage of coercion and violence. To proclaim Jesus as Lord is to live in the light of the resurrection, knowing that death does not have the final word.

3. *The church is our first family:* Though a Christian's deepest identity is rooted in a transcendent reality, we do continue to live in the world of time and space. Faith is always embodied in particular social forms, cultural rituals, economic relationships, and political structures. Very often these forms of cultural expression overwhelm the spiritual essence they are embracing. Without realizing it,

Christians frequently find themselves worshiping the form, be it money, power, or the nation, rather than the spirit these forms are to embody. For the Christian, the church is the primary point of identity.

As the living body of Christ, Christians gather as a community of faith to remember God's acts in history, to confess their sins, to offer praise to God. The mere fact of the church's existence—as a social body committed to a cause that transcends social, economic, and political boundaries—is a proclamation that Christ's reign is breaking into the world.

4. God's love is good news for the world: The gospel is good news not only for those who have accepted God's love and forgiveness, but also for those who are still living in fear, thinking that reality is grounded in selfishness and coercion. Christ's way of peace is genuine *news* for those who are trapped in a worldview of violence, and it is genuinely *good* because it invites each person to a life of trust and love, grounded in the generous love of God.

5. We are participants in God's invitation to Shalom: The invitation to become a Christian begins with a change of heart, a new way of looking at reality itself. But that change of heart is truly meaningful only to the extent that it engages us in the concrete and tangible acts of Shalom. As members of Christ's body and as citizens of many countries, we are each called to participate in God's plan for humans to live together in harmony—honoring the dignity of each person, celebrating the many expressions of God's image, promoting the cause of peace and justice, and in all things "seeking the welfare of the city."

CONCLUSION

For all of these reasons, Christians should choose against war.

The adventurous journey of faith offers no guarantees about how the world will react to the Christian witness to compassion, vulnerability, and love. But we can claim the power of the resurrection. We can celebrate even now the fact that death will not have the final word. And we can testify with joy that God's love is indeed stronger than our fear.

FOR FURTHER READING

There is a vast and growing literature on Christian peacemaking and the gospel of peace. The references cited below represent only a small sampling of this rich bibliography. More information on most of the organizations mentioned in the text can be readily found on the World Wide Web.

Biblical/Exegetical

Eller, Vernon. *War and Peace from Genesis to Revelation: King Jesus' Manual of Arms for the 'Armless* (Scottdale, PA: Herald Press, 1981). Suggests that peace is a central motif in the entire biblical story, both Old Testament and New Testament.

Klassen, William. *Love of Enemies* (Philadelphia: Fortress Press, 1984). An overview of the biblical themes of peace, with special attention to the Old Testament and intertestamental periods.

McSorley, Richard. *New Testament Basis of Peacemaking* (Washington, DC: Georgetown University, Center for Peace Studies, 1979). A Catholic defense, in simple and clear language, of Christ's call to peace and a refutation of Just War arguments.

Yoder, John Howard. *The Politics of Jesus: Vicit Agnus Noster,* 2nd ed. (Grand Rapids, MI: Eerdmans, 1999). A classic text offering a New Testament basis for the relevance of Christian pacifism.

Theological

Brown, Dale W. *Biblical Pacifism: A Peace Church Perspective* (Elgin, IL: Brethren Press, 1986). A survey of contemporary pacifist positions informed by biblically-based strategies for peacemaking.

Cahill, Lisa Sowle. *Love Your Enemies: Discipleship, Pacifism and Just War Theory* (Minneapolis: Fortress Press, 1994). A theological examination of the theory of Just War and the practice of pacifism from the perspective of a Catholic ethicist.

Clouse, Robert G. *War: Four Christian Views* (Downers Grove, IL: InterVarsity Press, 1981). A snapshot perspective on various attitudes toward war and peace in the Christian tradition.

Sider, Ron. *Christ and Violence* (Scottdale, PA: Herald Press, 1979). Sets forth a biblical basis for pacifism in which peace is central to salvation.

Personal Stories

Arnold, Johann Christoph. *Why Forgive?* (Farmington, PA: The Plough Publishing House, 2000). A collection of powerful stories of victims whose paths to healing came through forgiveness.

Gish, Arthur G. *Hebron Journal: Stories of Nonviolent Peacemaking* (Scottdale, PA: Herald Press, 2001). A personal perspective on the challenges of peacemaking in the Middle East.

Peachey, Titus and Linda Gehman Peachey, eds. *Seeking Peace* (Intercourse, PA: Good Books, 1991). Stories of individuals who attempted, sometimes at great cost, to live out their beliefs in peace.

Applied Peacemaking

Herr, Robert and Judy Zimmerman Herr, eds. *Transforming Violence: Linking Local and Global Peacemaking* (Scottdale, PA: Herald Press, 1998). An ecumenical collection of insights on peacemaking by Christians in Africa, Asia, Europe, and North America.

Sampson, Cynthia and John Paul Lederach. *From the Ground Up: Mennonite Contributions to International Peacemaking* (Oxford: Oxford University Press, 2000). Case studies on peacemaking and conflict resolution that link spirituality with pragmatic efforts at international peacebuilding.

Stassen, Glen, ed. *Just Peacemaking. Ten Practices for Abolishing War* (Cleveland, OH: Pilgrim Press, 1998). Specific and practical suggestions for moving toward a more peaceful world.

ABOUT
THE AUTHOR

John D. Roth was born and
raised in Holmes County, Ohio.
In 1989 he received his Ph.D. in
Early Modern European History
from the University of Chicago.
Since 1988 he has taught in the
history department at Goshen
College (Goshen, IN).

In addition to teaching, Roth
also serves as the editor of *The
Mennonite Quarterly Review*, an
academic journal focusing on
Anabaptists, Hutterites, Mennonites, and Amish. His
research and publications have concentrated primarily on
topics related to the Radical Reformation.

He and his wife, Ruth, are the parents of four children
and are actively involved in the life of their local congregation.